MAINE

BEER

Brewing in Vacationland

Josh Christie

AMERICAN PALATE

Published by The History Press
Charleston, SC 29403
www.historypress.net

Front cover, top: Photo courtesy of flickr user Guillén Pérez.
Back cover, top left: Photo by author. *Top right*: Photo courtesy of Kennebec River Brewing
Company. *Bottom left*: Photo courtesy of Michael Donk, brewbokeh.com.

First published 2013

Manufactured in the United States

ISBN 978.1.60949.683.8

Library of Congress CIP data applied for.

Notice: The information in this book is true and complete to the best of our knowledge. It is
offered without guarantee on the part of the author or The History Press. The author and
The History Press disclaim all liability in connection with the use of this book.

Contents

CONTENTS

Acknowledgements

T hanks to The History Press, and Whitney Tarella Landis in particular, for taking a chance on a freelance beer writer and bringing me on to write this book.

Thanks to all the folks in the Maine beer business, be they brewers, distributors, bartenders or consumers, for spreading the good beer gospel and giving Maine one of the best beer scenes in the country. Brewers were generous with their time and their input as I pulled this project together.

Though plenty of this book was crafted from primary research and interviews, a huge debt is owed to the authors who covered Maine beer before I did. Andy Crouch's *Good Beer Guide to New England*, Norman Miller's *Beer Lover's New England* and Will Anderson's *The Great State of Maine Beer Book* were—and still are—invaluable resources.

Thanks to Joe Grant and Deirdre Fleming at the *Maine Sunday Telegram*; Josh Flanagan, Conor Kilpatrick and Ron Richards at iFanboy; and Joseph Tucker at RateBeer.com for getting me started as a writer, both in print and on the web. Along those same lines, I owe my gratitude to my colleagues at all those publications for acting as editors and sounding boards.

Thanks to the staff at the Maine State Library and the Glickman Library for preserving information about the history of our great state. Thanks as well to the Portland Historical Society and the Maine Memory Network for their extensive catalogs of photographs and historical documents.

Finally, thanks to all of my family and friends for their support. I owe particular thanks to my wife, Katrina. Katy went from my girlfriend to fiancée to wife over the course of this book and was blessedly patient with both the time I devoted to this project and the anxiety of a first-time author. She certainly deserves credit as my most ardent copyeditor.

Author's Note

The information in *Maine Beer: Brewing in Vacationland* is, to the best of my knowledge, accurate and current. As you'll find in this guide, the landscape of Maine beer is constantly changing and evolving. I encourage you to reach out to the included breweries via the phone numbers and websites provided before visiting if you have any questions.

Introduction

B efore I started writing this book, I never knew how good I had it as a beer drinker in Maine.

By the time I turned twenty-one, Maine beer was already well established. Allagash Brewing Company had just celebrated its tenth anniversary in 2006, and David Geary was celebrating two decades of brewing Maine's flagship Pale Ale. Maine had twenty-three breweries when I tipped my first legal pint, and the number has only grown in the following years. Belgian ales, imperial stouts, IPAs, English bitters...not only did practically every Maine bar seem to have good beer, but a lot of it was also brewed right here in the state.

Maine beer is fantastic, and Maine's brewery culture is booming. Case closed, right?

It wasn't always this way. The Pine Tree State's relationship with beer— and alcohol in general—has been complicated, to say the least. The temperance movement found an early foothold in Maine, and Mainers (led by Portland's infamous Colonel Neal Dow) passed a law prohibiting the sale or manufacture of alcohol in 1851. Legal beer already had been out of Maine for over seven decades by the time national Prohibition kicked in in 1920. State and national Prohibition didn't stop a few enterprising individuals from brewing, but it certainly kept Maine from developing much of a beer culture.

As I look at the nearly forty breweries and brewpubs in the state today, it's hard to believe we ever had anything but a slobbering love affair with ales and lagers. Maine has emerged from the chains of Prohibition to create a beer culture that rivals any other in the United States. From early pioneers who established the Northeast's love affair with English-style ales to upstarts brewing extreme or long-dead recipes, Maine brewers create beer for every palate. Our state is home to some of the largest (Shipyard), fastest-growing (Baxter) and best-reviewed (Allagash) breweries in the nation.

In *Maine Beer: Brewing in Vacationland*, I've attempted to profile every operating brewery in Maine, along with a number of the state's brewpubs. Each profile follows a similar format, beginning with an in-depth look at the history and personalities at each brewery and followed by a brief profile of

The seal of the State of Maine, featuring the state motto "Dirigo" (or I Lead). *From Hugo Gerard Ströhl's* 1899 Heraldischer Atlas.

the brewer's best beers. Where applicable, a "What's in a Name?" section looks at the stories behind the sometimes historical, sometimes humorous and always interesting names of Maine's beers and breweries. For those looking to raise a glass to Maine breweries past and present, the book ends with appendices listing the state's now-defunct brewers and the state's best places to sit and enjoy a pint.

Maine's culture has always been one of fierce independence, and this spirit is seen in the dozens of Maine brewers and brewery founders. The indomitable spirit of Maine has created some serious characters, to be sure. Some trained for decades in traditional breweries before establishing their brands in Maine, and some jumped in feet first with hardly a batch of homebrew under their belt. Some run small nanobreweries that only brew beer for their local communities, while behemoths like Shipyard fill six thousand cases of beer a day.

As I was researching *Maine Beer: Brewing in Vacationland*, I found myself consistently returning to the Maine state motto—*Dirigo*. Latin for "I Lead," Maine's motto suggests that the state guides its citizens toward the loftiest patriotism. It is also sometimes interpreted as Mainers setting the course other United States' citizens follow. Maine didn't just lead the nation's charge into temperance; the state has also led—and continues to lead—the craft beer revolution.

Maine Beer: A Brief History

During its early days as a state—and earlier days as a part of the Commonwealth of Massachusetts—Maine's relationship with alcohol was no different than its neighbors in New England. It was, quite simply, a part of daily life.

To the sensibilities of modern Americans, our colonial ancestors seem like positive lushes. Reports of life in the 1770s suggest that the average adult white man drank the equivalent of seven shots of hard alcohol every day. Women weren't far behind, with the average white woman putting away about two pints of hard cider daily. Drinking wasn't purely the domain of the home or tavern, either—colonials drank at work, in church, in court and in public areas. Even the children of the American colonies were known to drink ale.

So, why all the drinking in early Maine? One reason for the liberal drinking was simply safety. Water wasn't purified; fresh water was filled with everything from insects to animal blood, and there was no guarantee that it wouldn't make drinkers violently ill. The same safety warnings went for milk, since colonial cows' diets could leave drinkers with "milk sickness." When colonists drank non-alcoholic beverages, there was a serious danger of catching water-borne illnesses like cholera.

The boiling of water (to brew beer) and the growth of yeast (to ferment beer) killed off the dangerous bacteria found in fresh water. Not only that, but the alcohol in beer—as well as liquor and wine—meant that alcoholic beverages could be stored for months without spoiling. Men, women and children didn't drink early American ales to admire the delicate balance of hops and malt. They drank for the practical purpose of safety.

Despite the drinking habits of early Americans, public drunkenness wasn't an immediate concern. Drinking wasn't done in evening-time binges, but throughout the day, every day. Despite occasional reports of drunkenness in early Maine newspapers, drinking wasn't the scourge it would later become. The old idea of "everything in moderation," so often applied to alcohol in modern times, was a way of life in the late 1700s and early 1800s.

Alcohol was so ingrained in the early American psyche that soldiers in the Revolutionary army received a ration of alcohol. Starting in 1781, members of the Revolutionary army received a daily ration of government-supplied rum. This shift, which moved the earliest Mainers' drinking habits from ale and cider to distilled spirits, may have marked the beginning of the state's bigger problems with alcohol.

As the eighteenth century ended, newly liberated Americans established farms all over the south and west of the United States. These farms produced a lot of corn, and early distillers discovered that they could turn a tidy profit changing that grain into whiskey. Distilled spirits flowed to the northeast, and drinking hit unprecedented levels—about seven gallons of pure alcohol per citizen every year. Among the heavy drinkers of the early 1800s, the people of Maine may have drunk the most.

With a population of hard-living fishermen, lumbermen, millworkers and farmers, Maine had citizens that drank more than anyone else in the country. Along with the ever-popular local ale and cider, whiskey flowed in from the west, and rum came to Maine ports from the Caribbean. In Portland—a town of fewer than ten thousand—there were about six hundred places to buy alcohol by the turn of the century. Many grocers' shops even kept rum punch prepared in a tub, sometimes on the sidewalk, according to early accounts of the city. The ugly side of alcohol abuse began to rear its head, and rates of violence, spousal and child abuse and loss of work rose precipitously.

This dangerous jump in drunkenness was mirrored by the rest of the country, and Maine's citizens were at the forefront of a national temperance movement. In 1815, the nation's first Total Abstinence Society was founded in Portland. Unlike temperance societies, which promoted moderation and reduction in alcohol consumption, the Total Abstinence Society advocated for complete renunciation of alcohol.

Maine's best-known crusader against alcohol was Neal S. Dow. Nicknamed the "Napoleon of Temperance" and the "Father of Prohibition," the Maine

General Neal Dow, mayor of Portland and architect of the prohibitionary Maine Law. He was known as the "Napoleon of Temperance." *Courtesy of the Library of Congress, LC-USZ62-90764.*

native laid much of the early groundwork for both state and national prohibition. The son of Quakers, Neal's opposition to alcohol was a major theme in his life. After high school, he joined his father's tanning business, and he wasn't shy about his opposition to his fellow employees' heavy drinking. Dow didn't attend the already-prestigious Bowdoin College for fear of the moral corruption he would experience there. When he reached the age at which he'd be obligated to join the militia, he joined Portland's volunteer fire department instead—largely to avoid the hard-drinking habits of the militia. Once there, Dow convinced the company to forgo liquor at its annual bash.

In his memoir *Reminiscences*, Dow succinctly put forth his view of the prevailing attitudes toward alcohol in early Maine.

> *The prevalent opinion that liquor was a panacea for all complaints, a protection in all forms of exposure, a relief for fatigue and pain, and for all other discomforts incident to hard labor and extremes of heat and cold, made its use general among fishermen and lumbermen…the excitement of drink took the place of the comforts of life, and, the appetite being thus*

created, excess naturally followed...The boys imitated the elders, until indulgence in drink almost everywhere was the rule.

Dow's anti-alcohol views gained him plenty of fans in Maine's growing temperance movement. This coincided with a change in the aims of many teetotalers. If efforts to change views were failing, why not just change the laws that govern them?

In the span of a few short decades, prohibitionary laws gained plenty of traction in Maine. An 1837 law proposing statewide prohibition made it out of committee in the Maine legislature but died soon after. Then, in 1846, with pressure from the state's temperance societies, Maine enacted a statewide law banning the sale of spirits and wine in small quantities. Though Dow was initially thrilled, the law ended up being laughably weak. The only penalty for those selling spirits was a small fine if violators were successfully prosecuted, and many local governments refused to even enforce the law.

Dow was so upset by the failure of the 1846 measure that he decided to enter Maine politics. If he couldn't change the law by lobbying Maine politicians, he would change the law while in office. With the support of the city's ardent Prohibitionists, Dow was elected mayor of Portland in April 1851. Once in office, the Father of Prohibition wasted no time. He worked with Maine legislators in May to draft a tougher anti-liquor law, which prohibited the production and sale of alcohol in Maine (with an exception for "medicinal or mechanical" use). Anyone who sold liquor would be fined, and anyone who manufactured liquor would be jailed.

The legislature moved fast in those days. Less than two months after Dow's election, the "Maine Law" was on Governor John Hubbard's desk. On June 2, Maine became the nation's first totally dry state. Mayor Dow gave liquor dealers in Portland sixty days to get rid of any of their remaining stock—on day sixty-one, he was coming after them.

The Maine Law

A statewide law calling for a total ban on the manufacture and sale of liquor was the first of its kind, and supporters of temperance saw it as a model statute. While we now see that total prohibition (of alcohol or anything else) is almost never successful, the view at the time was a bit rosy. In a *New York Times* editorial from October 1851, the paper of record painted Portland as a utopian city, free of the danger of "strong drink."

The Temperance banner is unfurled with new devices blazoned upon it, in some of our cities and throughout our entire State. A remarkable spectacle can be seen in the streets of the city of Portland. Temperate men, and nothing but temperate men, walk her streets. No places are open to sell strong drink, and there are no visible signs of intoxication. A strange quiet prevails. The clamor, and rioting, and fierce turbulence of drunkenness are nowhere seen. It is strange. Probably in no other State can just this condition of things be found. What a noble spectacle, could the eye be gladdened always by the sight of even one city thoroughly redeemed from the curse inflicted by strong drink.

Emboldened by the passage of the Maine Law, a number of other states followed suit. Between 1851 and 1855, Massachusetts, Vermont, Connecticut, Indiana, Michigan, Ohio, New York, Pennsylvania, Iowa and New Hampshire also passed so-called Maine Laws, completely prohibiting the sale of liquor. The passage of these laws wasn't always easy—many were overturned in their earliest forms as unconstitutional— but they showed the strength of a growing temperance movement that would lead to national Prohibition decades later.

Despite the popularity of the movement around the United States, all was not well in the Pine Tree State. Going from the nation's "drunkest" state to its driest in a single piece of legislation wasn't an easy move for many Mainers. Of course, a number of Mainers just kept on drinking. Some simply

TREE of INTEMPERANCE

BY A.D. FILLMORE.

The "Tree of Intemperance," expounding on the benefits of temperance and the evils of drink. One of the men below the tree holds a banner that reads "Hurrah! for the Maine Law." *Courtesy of the Library of Congress, LC-USZ62-14614.*

worked within loopholes in the Maine Law. Since the law didn't explicitly prohibit the consumption of alcohol (just the sale and manufacture), Maine restaurateurs would sell expensive snacks and toss in an alcoholic drink on the house. The Maine Law's exception for "medicinal alcohol" saw Maine physicians lining their pockets with profits from alcohol prescriptions. Other enterprising Mainers were bootleggers, bringing alcohol into the state across its porous borders or along its long coast.

Particularly fierce opposition to the Maine Law came from Maine's immigrant population—specifically Portland's Irish immigrants. At the time the Maine Law was enacted, about a tenth of Portland's population was Irish-born. The immigrants had a contentious relationship with Mayor Dow; they saw his prohibition law as an attack on their heritage, and he saw the population as responsible for the city's hard-drinking habits.

The antagonistic relationship came to a head on June 2, 1855, the fourth anniversary of the Maine Law. Word spread among Portland's residents that Dow had a cache of alcohol stored in the vaults underneath city hall. Though this liquor was meant for perfectly legal distribution to Maine's pharmacists and doctors, rumors circulated that Dow was planning on selling the liquor. Throughout the day, protestors gathered on the steps of city hall. The largely Irish crowd, which numbered in the thousands, grew restless as the day stretched on. Around 8:00 p.m., the crowd surged, throwing rocks and attempting to force their way into the city's vaults. A panicked Dow called in the Maine militia and eventually ordered that they fire on the crowd. By the time the media-dubbed "Portland Rum Riot" ended, one protestor was dead, and several police, protestors and innocent bystanders were injured.

In the aftermath of the riot, the pendulum of prohibition swung back; in 1856, the Maine Law was repealed, and a law allowing limited sale of alcohol as a beverage was put into place. Maine tap-danced around prohibition for decades, strengthening or weakening rules and enforcement. Prohibition grew to its strongest since the Maine Law in 1885, when an amendment was added to the state's constitution outlawing the sale or manufacture of alcoholic beverages.

My favorite beer-related story from this prohibitionary period concerns the McGlinchy brothers and their breweries. James "Handsome Jim" McGlinchy, an Irishman who came to Portland in 1840, operated the last breweries in the Portland area during prohibition with his brother Patrick. In November 1858, the two opened the Forest City Brewery at what is now the corner of Highland Avenue and Ocean Street in South Portland. In January 1861, they opened the Casco Brewery on Fore Street in Portland. The two

THE LAST BUILDING USED AS A BREWERY IN MAINE.

The Casco Brewery, located on Portland's Munjoy Hill on Fore Street. The caption reads, "THE LAST BUILDING USED AS A BREWERY IN MAINE." *Courtesy of the Collections of Maine Historical Society.*

breweries managed to operate throughout Maine's turbulent prohibition environment thanks to a reliable loophole—they were able to brew beer, as long as it was produced for sale outside of the state. There's little doubt that the beer managed to find its way into the mugs of Mainers as well.

A handful of delightful ads for the breweries ran in Portland's paper of record, the *Daily Eastern Argus*. They show that the breweries offered a full complement of ales in the styles of pale, amber, cream and porter. An 1861 ad for the Forest City Brewery includes sworn testimony from a Massachusetts state assayer that the brewery's offerings have "the essential qualities found in the best [beer], either foreign or domestic." Perhaps looking to thread one of Maine's prohibition loopholes, an 1871 ad from the Casco Brewery ends with the note that "we would respectfully call the attention of invalids where ALE is recommended by physicians."

By the end of the 1800s, brewing had dried up in Maine. Maine's prohibition laws chugged along, and temperance laws rose and fell around the country. In the larger view, there was, inexorably, movement in a single direction. In the

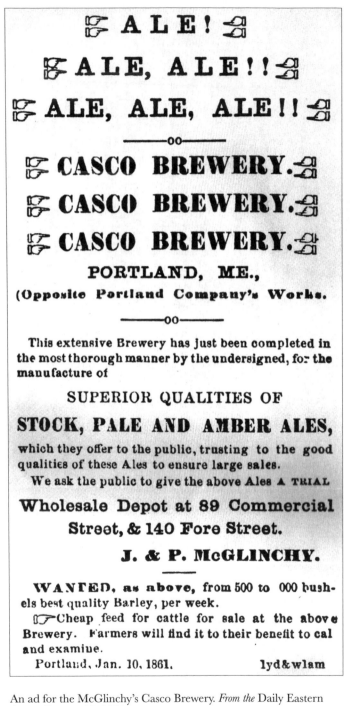

An ad for the McGlinchy's Casco Brewery. *From the* Daily Eastern Argus, *January 10, 1861.*

early days of the twentieth century, state after state fell into the "dry" column alongside Maine. Years of temperance-led education had raised a generation of Americans convinced of the evils of alcohol. The First World War was the final straw, with anti-German furor cementing opposition to the German immigrants behind many of the country's biggest breweries.

The Eighteenth Amendment, establishing prohibition of alcoholic beverages in the United States, was submitted to the states by Congress on December 18, 1917. It was ratified on January 16, 1919, and went into effect one year later.

As goes Maine, so goes the nation. Nearly seventy years after Maine went dry, the rest of the nation followed suit.

PROHIBITION

In a beer history of Maine, there's little to report during the thirteen years of America's "Noble Experiment" with national prohibition. By that point, Mainers had been dealing with alcohol prohibition of one kind or another for more than half a century. Maine's breweries had already been shuttered for decades when the Eighteenth Amendment and the Volstead Act (the enforcement mechanism for Prohibition) kicked in. Most of the alcohol that was illegally produced in Maine or passed through its borders was liquor, a more potent and profitable commodity than beer. The thirteen years of Prohibition saw occasional reports of smuggled beer in the *Bangor Daily News*, *Lewiston Daily Sun* and *Portland Press Herald*, but liquor enforcement busts were dominated by rum and whiskey.

That said, Maine wasn't totally free of brewers during the years of national Prohibition. In her excellent oral history of Brunswick during Prohibition, Judy Laster notes that Bowdoin students brewed their own beer in fraternity basements. It's suggested that fraternities at other Maine universities followed suit, and there's little doubt that frat parties from Orono to Lewiston featured house-brewed beer.

National Prohibition worked as well in Maine as statewide prohibition had; it kept people from drinking as well as a sieve held water. Enforcement wasn't any more successful in the rest of the nation, and public sentiment toward legislated temperance soured. With the famous line "I think this would be a good time for a beer," President Franklin Roosevelt signed an amendment to the Volstead Act allowing for the sale of light beer and wines in March 1933. This was followed by the state-by-state ratification of the Twenty-first Amendment.

A cache of liquor being taken off a ship in Portland Harbor at Grand Trunk Wharf in 1920 when Prohibition was in effect. *Courtesy of the Collections of Maine Historical Society.*

Maine was the thirty-seventh state to approve of the amendment at a special state ratifying convention. The *New York Times* of December 7, 1933, reported:

Maine Ratifies Repeal, But State Stays Dry
AUGUSTA, Me., Dec. 6.—Maine's constitutional convention today voted unanimously for repeal of the Eighteenth Amendment to the Federal Constitution, but the State remains in its long-time dry status through a stringent prohibitory article to its Constitution and companion statutes.

The Legislature, now in special session, is expected to act on proposals for immediate regulated and controlled sale of hard liquor for medicinal and mechanical purposes and the "arts," permissible under the State prohibitory amendment.

Maine was one of the final states to get on board with the amendment—the ratification of the proposed amendment by Ohio, Pennsylvania and Utah the day before had given it the necessary votes to be enacted. Still, the ratification by the stridently anti-alcohol Maine was symbolically important.

By 1930, national groups like the Crusaders had organized to repeal the Eighteenth Amendment. *Courtesy of the Library of Congress, LC-USZ62-72992.*

With the passage of the Twenty-first Amendment, national Prohibition was over. People could once again drink openly, and breweries could finally get back to the business of fermentation.

AFTER PROHIBITION

While the Cullen-Harrison Act kicked in on April 7, 1933 (allowing for the sale of beer 4 percent ABV or less), the law only affected states that had amended their own laws to legalize alcohol sales. Mainers didn't get to sip on beer on "New Beer's Eve" with the twenty states that had allowed for legal beer, as they hadn't yet repealed Maine's long-standing state prohibition laws. But they didn't need to wait long—within a year, statewide repeal passed and alcohol was legal in Maine. On the first of July 1934, beer once again flowed into Maine.

Though beer was now (legally) in the hands of Maine drinkers, beer culture in the United States had changed drastically. Only the largest breweries, which had been able to pivot from beer production to other goods like cola and near beer during Prohibition, had survived a decade and a half of "dry" United States. The United States' entry into World War II squelched any real hopes of upstart brewers gaining ground. In Maine and around the country, grain was rationed—a move that drove a number of upstarts out of business and led to big brewers like Anheuser-Busch and Coors Brewing Company cutting their traditional malted barley with corn and rice. These established brewers were able to convince the U.S. government of the health (and tax) benefits of beer sales, a ploy that worked so well they were asked to set 15 percent of their production aside for servicemen.

It may have been the move that cemented the role of huge industrial brewers and light lager as American staples. Brewers of watered-down, mass-produced lagers—Anheuser-Busch, Pabst, Schlitz and others—grew with little competition, and huge numbers of soldiers returned home with affection for the beer they received as rations overseas.

Maine had beer in the decades following the war, but none of it was the state's own (and none of it particularly good). It was almost exclusively Budweiser and Miller stuff—Coors didn't make it to Maine until the '90s. A handful of outfits in Southern Maine lobbied the state for brewing licenses but never actually got around to brewing any beer. In the 1970s, small craft breweries like California's New Albion and Sierra Nevada started popping up, but Maine's historical record doesn't show any successes

Though Mainers could drink freely once again after the repeal of Prohibition, the beer landscape had shifted from many local breweries to a handful of regional and national concerns. *Courtesy of the Library of Congress, LC-USF34-042601-D.*

Maine drinkers, like these shipyard workers in 1940s Bath, wouldn't have any local options for beer until decades later. *Courtesy of the Library of Congress, LC-USF34-042598-D.*

or failures in Maine—it seems no one even tried to open a brewery here. President Jimmy Carter's legalization of homebrewing in 1978 planted the first seeds of brewing in Mainers' minds. Though the state was years from having a commercial brewery of its own, at least residents were able to start experimenting with ale on a small scale.

One important step toward fermenting a beer revolution in Maine was creating the legal framework for breweries to exist in the state. The passage of LD 1579—An Act Concerning the Licensing of Small Maine Breweries—in the spring of 1985 started to put this framework into place.

An Act Concerning the Licensing of Small Maine Breweries.
Be it enacted by the People of the State of Maine as follows:
28 MRSA §501, sub-§1-A is enacted to read:
1-A. Small Maine breweries. Small Maine breweries shall pay an annual license fee of…$50.

For purposes of this section, "small Maine brewery" means a facility that is brewing, lagering and kegging, bottling or packaging its own malt liquors within the State. If an inadequate amount of agricultural products used for raw materials exists within the State, a holder of a small Maine brewery license may file an affidavit and application with the Bureau of Alcoholic Beverages setting forth the unavailability of raw materials within the State and requesting permission to import those agricultural products from out-of-state. If the bureau finds that there is in fact an inadequate supply of raw materials within the state, it may authorize that importation.

A holder of a small Maine brewery license may produce malt liquors containing 25% or less alcohol by volume in an amount not to exceed 50,000 gallons per year, or their metric equivalent.

A holder of a small Maine brewery license may sell, on the premises during regular business hours, malt liquors produced at the brewery by the bottle, case or in bulk.

A holder of a small Maine brewery license may sell or deliver his product to licensed retailers and wholesalers. In addition, he may sell, on the premises for consumption off the premises, malt liquors produced at the brewery by the bottle, case or in bulk to licensed retailers, including, but not limited to, retail stores, restaurants and clubs.

A holder of a small Maine brewery license may apply for one license for the sale of liquor for on-premise consumption for a location other than the brewery.

Maine Beer: A Brief History

A holder of a small Maine brewery license may list on product labels and in its advertising the list of the ingredients and the product's average percentage of the recommended daily allowances of nutritional requirements.

More than simply a law that allowed folks to brew professionally in Maine, LD 1579 laid out limits on production and alcohol levels and allowed for self-distribution and on-premises service and sales (a crucial piece for brewpubs).

The law was created largely due to the urging of Henry Cabot, the owner of a Waldoboro restaurant named the Pine Cone Public House. Cabot wanted to expand his restaurant into a brewpub. Though Cabot's business is now consigned to history, his efforts created an environment where the Maine beer scene could be born.

By the time the law passed in 1985, beer from craft breweries in the United States and abroad had started to arrive in Maine. A handful of bars, like Portland's Three Dollar Dewey's, grew the Maine palate to look for beer more complex than light American lagers. All the state needed, it seemed, was a brewery to call its own—the first since the McGlinchy brothers' Portland breweries closed over a century before.

Vacationland didn't need to wait for long. In December 1986, the D.L. Geary Brewing Company sold its first beer, kicking off a brewing renaissance that continues to this day.

D.L. Geary Brewing Company

38 Evergreen Drive, Portland | (207) 878-2337
www.gearybrewing.com | Founded 1984

THE BREWERY

D.L. Geary Brewing Company is probably one of the main reasons we have so many great craft breweries here in Maine. The brewery opened in 1986, when there were only about a dozen microbreweries in the United States. Both D.L. and the brewery have been pioneering forces in the American brewing world and paved the way (and prepared the taste buds of Mainers) for the score of craft brewers in the state today.

The story of the brewery (popularly known as simply "Geary's") starts in the early '80s. After conversations with Three Dollar Dewey's founder Alan Eames, David Geary and his wife, Karen, found themselves convinced of the viability of a brewery based in Portland, Maine. Eames introduced Geary to Peter Maxwell Stuart, owner of Scotland's famous Traquair House Brewery. After Stuart heard of David's brewing aspirations, he didn't just invite the Mainer to visit Traquair House—he offered Geary an apprenticeship. After touring Scotland, the United Kingdom's brewing world, in 1984, Geary came back to the states and founded the D.L. Geary Brewing Company with Karen Geary and brewmaster Alan Pugsley. With funding from 125 friends and neighbors, the business was born.

A 2007 shot of the interior of the Geary's brewhouse. *Photo courtesy of flickr user Cliff1066.*

Geary's, exterior. *Photo by the author.*

When it sold its first beer in December 1986, Geary's was Maine's first brewery in over a century. Not only that, but its existence brought the number of craft breweries in the United States up to just a baker's dozen. As one of the first breweries on the market, it fell on Karen, David and Alan to explain their beer and get it into people's hands. Though it's unquestionably tough for any brewery starting today, it's hard to imagine how difficult it was when there was no one available to offer advice and share supplies and no one else's mistakes to learn from.

In twenty-five years, a lot has changed for D.L. Geary—both the brewery and the man. Karen and David split up in 1989, though they continue to work together at the brewery. While it hasn't experienced the explosive growth of some of its contemporaries, Geary's is available in at least a dozen states, and the eighteen-thousand-square-foot brewery brews about eighteen thousand barrels a year. A planned expansion will add another fifteen thousand square feet. A few perks of the expansion will be an increase in brewing days (up to seven days a week), twenty-two-ounce "bomber" bottles and even contract brewing for other Maine breweries.

THE BEER

The brewery's flagship beer, **Geary's Pale Ale**, is a classic British pale ale with some tangy fruitiness from an imported Hampshire yeast strain. It remains the brewery's most popular beer, with good reason—it's essentially the platonic ideal of the pale ale that exists at nearly every English-styled craft brewery in the Northeast.

The year-round brews from D.L. are rounded out by the popular **HSA Strong Ale** and **London Porter**, the winner of a *New York Times* blind taste test a few years back. For years, the omnipresent style of IPA was noticeably absent from the brewery's line—instead, the seasonal **Winter Ale** fit into that style. Things have been retooled a bit, with the new year-round **Geary's IPA** in the mix and a Winter Ale styled more after a bitter.

Geary's **Summer Ale** is one of its most popular beers, a seasonal ale based on the German kolsch. Not only does the beer taste great, but the bottle always looks fantastic. Every year, Geary's awards a $5,000 scholarship to the Maine College of Art student who submits the best design for the package and bottles.

Geary's has also jumped into the world of "big" beer in recent years, releasing two different four-packed imperial brews. The **Imperial IPA** and

Wee Heavy Scottish Ale are both big yet traditional beers, and the brewery has been smart about slowly introducing these beers to the market. Too many breweries seem to throw every beer they can at the wall to see what sticks, but D.L. Geary has seen steady growth by brewing just a few great beers.

WHAT'S IN A NAME?

One of my favorite discoveries during the research for this book was "InagurAle." The oddly named beer was brewed for the occasion of Governor Angus King's inaugural ball in 1995. It was Maine's first collaborative brew, made by the combined efforts of Geary and Gritty McDuff's brewmaster Ed Stebbins.

Here's how Ron Lachance described the special brew for beer periodical *Yankee Brew News*.

> *This ale was brewed "independently" by both breweries in order to commemorate the Independent Governor's recent victory at the polls. The brewers hoped that the spirit of co-operation displayed in the mutual production of this ale would help ease the memory of one of the most heated and closely watched elections in the State's history. What kind of beer does one brew for the newly elected Governor? Well, simply put, the brewers felt that the ale should somehow reflect Angus King's Scottish ancestry, and that it should taste...well...it should have the sweet taste of victory!*
>
> *With those premises in mind, Ed Stebbins and David Geary formulated a recipe for a Scotch Ale. They started with a mixture of imported two-row pale ale and crystal malt, and then added a generous amount of chocolate malt to darken the original extract. Yakima Cascade and Cluster hops were added to the boil in the kettle, and whole Oregon Willamette flowers were used as "finishing" hops.*

Gritty McDuff's Brewery

396 Fore Street, Portland (original brewpub) | (207) 772-BREW
www.grittys.com | Founded 1988

While D.L. Geary Brewing holds the title of the original Maine microbrewery, Gritty McDuff's Brewing Company has its own distinction as the state's first brewpub. Founded in 1988 by Ed Stebbins and Richard Pfeffer, the Gritty's on Fore Street in Portland was the first of many brewpubs hoping to bring a bit of the British publican culture to Maine's Old Port.

By 1986, just as Maine's beer revolution was starting, Gritty's co-founder Richard Pfeffer was toying with the idea of starting a brewpub. Pfeffer had a stockbroker job here in Maine, but his heart was in beer. The necessary ingredient to get Gritty McDuff's off the ground came in 1987, when Richard's college pal Ed Stebbins moved to Maine.

(Stebbins is perhaps the more recognizable of the co-founders—the happy bartender who adorned every Gritty's label for decades was a young Ed.)

Stebbins secured a loan from his grandmother to get the venture off the ground. Stebbins also apprenticed at the D.L. Geary Brewing Company, learning from Maine's brewing forefathers David Geary and Alan Pugsley. With a lease for a spot in Portland's Old Port and a seven-barrel brewing system purchased from Pugsley, Gritty McDuff's served its first pint of beer in December 1988. Three years after its first post-prohibition brewery, Maine had its first post-prohibition brewpub.

Image courtesy of Gritty McDuff's.

Gritty McDuff's founders Richard Pfeffer and Ed Stebbins, outside the Portland Brewpub. *Photo courtesy of Gritty McDuff's.*

Since opening that original pub on Fore Street in Portland, Gritty McDuff's has expanded. Pfeffer and Stebbins moved quickly, opening a new brewpub on Freeport's Main Street in 1994. Further expansion came a decade later, with a third Gritty McDuff's opening on the banks of Auburn's Androscoggin River in 2005. All three of the pubs are true brewpubs, housing brewing systems based on the popular Peter Austin model. If you get a pint on draft at any of the three locations, you can bet that it was brewed there. Bottled Gritty's beers come from a few different places—six-packs are contract brewed at Portland's Shipyard Brewery, but many of the twenty-two-ounce bottles and five-liter mini-kegs are brewed and packaged at the Freeport location.

At the Auburn, Freeport and Portland locations, Gritty McDuff's offers a fine selection of British and Atlantic fare—a hybrid of the hearty food of the United Kingdom and the local seafood flavor. All locations host live music and events, with a particularly busy schedule at the Portland location. And of course, in the tradition of great local watering holes everywhere, Gritty's has a mug club that'll net you extra beer and some pretty swank discounts, no matter which location you call home.

THE BEER

Like fellow local brewers Shipyard and Geary's, Gritty McDuff's sticks very closely to the classic British brew tradition. In Auburn and Freeport, the copper-topped, brick-faced brew kettles are based on designs from the Ringwood Brewery in Hampshire, England. Gritty's brews a handful of classic styles year-round (the **Best Bitter**, **Best Brown**, **Black Fly Stout**, **Pub Style** and often a **Pale** and a **Light**) and very traditional seasonal ales—each is simply a variation on a traditional English bitter. In recent years, McDuff's has experimented a bit more with U.S. styles, and the newest addition to its beer family is **Maine's Best IPA**, hopped with a very American blend of Cascade, Warrior and Willamette hops.

Gritty's has also had some success partnering with local businesses on special brews. The **Red Claws Ale** is a session amber paired with the Portland-based NBA Development Team of the same name. **Abram's Ale**, a winter seasonal, was first brewed to honor the fiftieth anniversary of Greenwood's Mount Abram Ski Resort. The Irish Red ale is served on a nitro tap, giving it the creamy head more often associated with a Guinness or Boddingtons.

WHAT'S IN A NAME?

I was a bit disappointed to find there's no fantastic story behind the name "Gritty McDuff." There's no great historical figure in Maine with that sobriquet. Gritty's co-founder Richard Pfeffer simply thought the name sounded good (and, more importantly, sounded British). "Gritty" was inspired by one of Pfeffer's high school buddies, and "McDuff" was conjured out of thin air. Despite some of the founder's early misgivings about the name, the catchy fabrication stuck.

Bar Harbor Brewing Company

8 Mount Desert Street, Bar Harbor | (207) 288-4592
www.barharborbrewing.com | Founded 1990

THE BREWERY

Maine's brewing revolution may have started in Portland with Gritty's and Geary's, but it quickly moved up the coast. In the first half of the '90s, more than half of the breweries opened in the state were in the Midcoast or Downeast. The first of these was the Bar Harbor Brewing Company.

Like a lot of craft beer fans, Tod Foster was a homebrewer when he was a college student. The California native, like many beer fans before him, also had dreams of one day opening his own brewery. After meeting his wife, native Mainer Suzi Murphy, the couple moved from the craft beer hub of the Pacific Northwest to Bar Harbor, Maine. The high start-up cost for brewery equipment initially kept Tod from going after his dream. This changed in late 1989, when Foster came across an ad for a small, two-barrel start-up system. Suddenly, opening a brewery seemed a bit more affordable.

Tod started brewing, and his first account was Doug Maffucci's New Old Lompoc Café. The Bar Harbor eatery, which served a few dozen bottled craft beers, started pouring Tod's creations in 1990. The café was the testing ground for Foster's first beer, Thunder Hole Ale. Looking to strike out on their own, Tod and Suzi built the Bar Harbor Brewing Company in the

150-square-foot basement of their home. Tod would brew the beer, and Suzi would handle the business side of things.

Growth was brisk enough that the brewery—and the Fosters—soon moved to a bigger space across town. The brewery remained in the Fosters' basement, but the square footage more than quintupled. In 1994, Bar Harbor Brewing upgraded from a two-barrel to a four-barrel brewing system. In the following decade, Tod and Suzi kept the brewery's growth restrained even as its reputation grew. In the late '90s, as both Thunder Hole Ale and Cadillac Mountain Stout took home gold medals at the World Beer Championships, they remained difficult to find outside of coastal Maine.

In the subsequent years, the brewery changed hands a couple times. Ad executive and developer Evan Contorakes purchased the brewery from the Fosters in 2008, keeping the founders on as consultants. The purchase meant big changes for the brewery: Bar Harbor Brewing moved to downtown Bar Harbor, production increased and some of its more popular brews (Cadillac Stout, Thunder Hole and Harbor Lighthouse) were contract-brewed at Geary's. The new arrangement didn't last long—in early 2009, the brewery sold again. Since then, the outfit has been owned by its former cross-town competitors Atlantic Brewing Company. It's a bit of a reunion—Doug Maffucci, whose café was the original home of Bar Harbor's beer, owns Atlantic.

Tod Foster, leading a tour at Bar Harbor Brewing Company. *Photo courtesy of flickr user Gandhirama.*

The new ownership has been good for the brewery. Bar Harbor's beers are now easy to find on store shelves and on draft, and the company's flagship brews have a taste much more faithful to their pre-Contorakes recipes.

THE BEER

The lineup of beers available from Bar Harbor Brewing Company has hardly changed in the decades it has been brewing. Through multiple owners and a couple different locations, the trifecta of **Thunder Hole Ale**, **Cadillac Mountain Stout** and **Harbor Lighthouse Ale** have been reliable finds on the Maine coast. A couple beers have been retired (Peach Ale, Ginger Mild Brew), and in the mid-2000s, the addition of **True Blue Blueberry Ale** brought the stable up to four.

Thunder Hole, a brown ale, was the brewery's first beer and remains its flagship ale. It's a faithful take on the English brown ale and is well regarded—the bottle boasts, "This is the brown ale that beat Newcastle, Sam Adams and more, at the World Beer Championships in Chicago." Harbor Lighthouse is a classic English mild, full-flavored but light in body and easy to session at only 3.2 percent ABV. True Blue is a standout in the crowded world of fruit beers, a copper-colored ale that doesn't lean too heavily on the blueberry flavor. Instead, a malt-and-wheat base is just barely kissed with blueberries.

The crown jewel of the Bar Harbor Brewing lineup is the Cadillac Mountain Stout, one of the best dry Irish stouts in the world. Chocolate and coffee flavors dominate this smooth-drinking beer, a silky treat with an aftertaste that goes on for days.

WHAT'S IN A NAME?

Most of the beers at the Bar Harbor Brewing Company take their names from attractions within Acadia National Park. Located on Mount Desert Island (as are the town of Bar Harbor and the brewery), Acadia was originally created as Lafayette National Park in 1919 but renamed Acadia in 1929. It was the first national park east of the Mississippi and remains one of the most popular.

Cadillac Mountain Stout and Thunder Hole Ale share their names with two popular attractions within Acadia, and the Harbor Lighthouse Ale is named after Bass Harbor Head Light.

Atlantic Brewing Company

15 Knox Road, Bar Harbor | (207) 288-2337
www.atlanticbrewing.com | Founded 1991

THE BREWERY

Doug Maffucci's path to Bar Harbor beverage baron began with a little restaurant called the New Old Lompoc Café. Doug and his partner Jon Hubbard, who already ran a bicycle shop and burger joint in Bar Harbor, decided to try their hands at a more substantial restaurant in 1989. The café's unique feature—its hook—was the beer selection. The New Old Lompoc Café would offer twenty-five bottled beers, all of them craft brews or imports. Though there were Maine beer bars that offered some choice in beer (namely, the Great Lost Bear and Three Dollar Dewey's in Portland), there wasn't anyplace offering this kind of choice in Bar Harbor. Even more unique was the allure of locally brewed beer. In 1990, the café was the first account for Tod and Suzi Foster's fledgling Bar Harbor Brewing Company.

When the Fosters went off to chart their own path with Bar Harbor Brewing, Doug started brewing beer himself. Maffucci launched Acadia Brewing Company in 1991, crafting beer one barrel at a time within the café. This grew to a full-scale brewpub, with a seven-barrel brewhouse attached to the eatery. In 1994, the brewery's name changed from Acadia to the now-familiar Atlantic Brewing Company.

A winter view of the Atlantic Brewing Company. Over the years, the small farmhouse has grown into a substantial estate brewery. *Photo courtesy of flickr user Cliff1066.*

Atlantic experienced steady growth in its early years and stayed strong even as the craft brewing bubble popped in the late '90s. The brewpub saw expansion after expansion, and in 1998, Maffucci moved Atlantic from downtown Bar Harbor to a farmhouse on the edge of town. The nineteenth-century Maine farmstead fit with the brewer's vision of an "estate brewery," replete with stonework and vegetation that brings to mind the beer gardens of Germany and England. The estate features Atlantic's production brewery, a gift shop and the Mainely Meat BBQ. While beer production is a year-round affair, visits to the estate are not—the brewery is only open to the public (excepting special appointments) from Memorial Day to Columbus Day.

In recent years, Maffucci's beverage empire (which he co-owns with his wife, Barbara Patten) has grown. In addition to beer, Atlantic crafts two different Maine sodas—a root beer and a blueberry soda. In 2004, Doug and Barbara opened a winery: Bar Harbor Cellars. In 2009, Atlantic Brewing Company acquired Bar Harbor Brewing Company, consolidating the island's brewing enterprises. As of 2012, Atlantic brews the equivalent of about fifty-five thousand cases of beer each year. The beer is brewed and bottled in two locations; some comes from the production brewery in Bar Harbor, and some is contract-brewed by Portland's Shipyard Brewing. With expanded distribution, upped production and a snazzy label redesign, Atlantic is poised to keep up its growth for another twenty years.

THE BEER

Love fruit beers? Thank Atlantic Brewing Company. When it introduced its **Blueberry Ale** in 1992, it was the first blueberry beer (and one of the first fruit beers) in the country. An amber ale with a strong but not overwhelming blueberry kick, it remains a classic take on the style.

Like a number of the pioneer breweries in New England, Atlantic's year-round lineup is dominated by beers based on classic English-style ales. **Bar Harbor Real Ale** and **Coal Porter** are faithful takes on the English brown and porter. The quirkier **Island Ginger** is a wheat ale brewed with twenty pounds of fresh ground ginger root in the boil. Though the light body of the wheat beer makes it popular among summer visitors, the spicy heat of the ginger also makes it a dynamite cold weather beer.

Atlantic's Blueberry Ale, born in 1992, has spawned dozens of imitators. *Image courtesy of Atlantic Brewing.*

In 2012, Atlantic added the long-absent style of IPA to its year-round bottled line. The **New Guy IPA** is a straightforward India Pale, brewed with pale malt and 100 percent Columbus hops. The end result is a straightforward beer that doesn't overwhelm the taste buds quite as much as some other IPAs.

Another recent addition to Atlantic's lineup is the Manly Man Beer Club, a series of small-batch beers that are usually high in alcohol and big on attitude. Offerings so far have included a wheat wine, double IPA, smoked barleywine and an ale brewed with molasses. They can be hit or miss—I think the wheat wine is a scattershot take on the style, but the smoked barleywine (**Sea Smoke**) is one of Maine's best beers. In a world where many of Maine's "first wave" of breweries are criticized for sticking too close to traditional English styles, Atlantic should be applauded for letting its talented brewers stretch their creative muscles.

WHAT'S IN A NAME?

While Atlantic's limited-release S.O.B. officially stands for "Special Old Bitter," the name was inspired by a curmudgeonly brewpub patron who better fit the acronym's more commonly known meaning. Brother Adam's Bragget, another limited release and one of the few braggots brewed in the United States, is named for Buckfast Abbey monk Brother Adams. A braggot is an English honey ale with roots in the 1300s, and Brother Adam—an Abbey beekeeper—is widely credited with saving the honeybee industry in the early twentieth century.

My favorite beer name in Atlantic's catalog is Ellen's Coffee Milk Stout, a delightful wintertime release brewed with lactose, coffee and vanilla. The name of the stout is a play on Allen's Coffee Brandy, perhaps Maine's most notorious liquor. The sweet, dark libation has been Maine's best-selling liquor for over two decades and often sells more than a million bottles in a single calendar year.

Andrew's Brewing Company

373 High Street, Lincolnville | (207) 763-3505
No Website Available | Founded 1992

THE BREWERY

If you're reading this book chronologically, you'll notice a collaborative pattern among Maine's brewers. It seems that Maine's brewers are all connected, be it by equipment, employment or simply advice. The trend continues with Andy Hazen, who needed a push from Bar Harbor Brewing Company's Tod and Suzi Foster to get his brewery off the ground.

An air force vet who settled on the coast of Maine, Hazen picked up the habit of homebrewing during the '80s. He started brewing for the same reason a lot of us did—as he told Will Anderson in *The Great State of Maine Beer Book*, homebrewing "was better and cheaper." As the decade wore on and Hazen's work started to thin (he worked as a carpenter), he started to seriously consider starting a commercial brewery. A visit to meet with the Fosters in Bar Harbor pushed Andy over the edge.

After a few years of planning, Hazen built a brewhouse in his Lincolnville home, usurping what had been in earlier lives a dairy farm and a woodworking shop. He was brewing on a half-barrel system by the end of '92, and his first beer sold on January 1, 1993. Within a month, Andrew's was adding commercial accounts. While the brewery never grew at an explosive pace, it gained a devoted following in Maine, particularly in the Midcoast region. Over the years, the brewery grew to a four-and-a-half-barrel system and eventually to an eleven-barrel system designed by Hazen and put together by a local welder.

For most of its life, Andrew's Brewing Company was a one-man operation. In this case, one-man meant not only "no other employees" but also "no mechanical assistance." Hazen brewed all his beer, hand-bottled and hand-labeled (or kegged) it all himself and packed the six-packs for distribution. Andrew's saw its employees double when Andy's son Ben returned home from a tour of duty in Iraq. The pair now act as partners, sharing both ownership and operation of the brewery.

Growth at Andrew's has been carefully managed over the years. The Hazens only produce a few different varieties of beer—three year-round brews and a seasonal—and share supply orders with other Maine breweries. Thanks to pairing with the distributor Pine State, Andrew's beer is now available all over Maine, and another distributor provides the brewery's beer to part of Vermont. Planned next steps for the brewery include the introduction of a winter seasonal, more "pilot" test batches brewed at the brewery and the possible introduction of growlers to be filled at the Lincolnville facility.

THE BEER

There's something to be said for doing one thing and doing it well. While the beer portfolios of other breweries that opened around the same time as Andrew's have ballooned in the following decades, Andrew's handful of offerings hasn't changed much. Like many other New England breweries, the Lincolnville brewer's flagship is a snappy **English Pale Ale**. It's a well-executed take on the style, jazzed up by the addition of the citrus flavor of some West Coast hops.

The rest of Andrew's lineup hews closely to traditional English style. The **Northern Brown Ale** is a nutty, caramel-tinged brew that will be instantly familiar to any fans of Newcastle, Samuel Smith or other sweet brown ales. **St. Nick's Porter** sticks to the original interpretation of a porter—it's not a stout stand-in, but a mild, chocolatey beer that fits snugly between sweeter mild ales and richer stouts.

The **Summer Golden Ale** is the brewery's lone seasonal brew. The highly aromatic blonde ale presents loads of grassy hops and bready malt scents over a light body. It's a well-brewed, highly drinkable beer, and the blonde ale presents an alternative to the wheat and pale ales that dominate summer seasonals.

Sunday River Brewing Company

1 Sunday River Road, Bethel | (207) 824-3541
www.sundayriverbrewpub.com | Founded 1992

THE BREWERY

Trust me when I say that it's hard to find a more beer-hungry demographic than Maine skiers. When they were trying to pick out a spot for their brewpub, cousins Grant Wilson and Hans Trupp found a perfect spot on Route 2 in Bethel. Right on the main thoroughfare to the popular ski area Sunday River, there was an empty cornfield. It wasn't for sale, technically speaking, but that didn't slow the pair down. They made an offer in March 1992, started construction of their brewpub in June and opened in December.

Peter Leavitt came on board, joining the crew as the pub's brewmaster. Leavitt came to Maine with four years of brewing experience, sporting credentials from the Siebel Institute for Brewing Studies in Chicago.

When the Sunday River Brewing Company (and pub, natch) opened in 1992, Sunday River was experiencing serious growth. The little brewery boomed along with the resort and grew into a strong enough brand that founder Grant Wilson started another operation, Stone Coast Brewing, in Portland just a few years later. Though Stone Coast boomed for a bit (and brewed a hell of a tasty bock), it eventually folded in 2008. More than two decades after its founding, Sunday River Brewing again stands alone.

Though Stone Coast Brewing Company is no longer around, the Sunday River pub offers some of the defunct brewer's beers—like the Jamaican Stout—on draft and in growlers. *Photo courtesy of flickr user walknboston.*

Perhaps the biggest benefit to come from Wilson's Stone Coast venture was Stewart Mason. Stewart (or "Stoo") came to Maine in 1997 when the Bethel brewery was expanding into Portland and has been in Maine since. Since the closure of Stone Coast, Mason has been the head brewer at Sunday River.

Though the pub has a fairly unassuming exterior, the inside is super cozy ski-chic. Booths and tables fill the floor of the restaurant, and some cafeteria-style tables sit by the fire for those cold January days. There's also a great bar with plenty of room to squeeze around. The brewpub has a decent menu, much improved over the last couple years and populated with burgers, chowders, chili and everything else that screams brewpub.

In terms of capacity, the Sunday River Brewing Company hummed along for years with a small-yet-efficient seven-barrel system. As Stone Coast grew in the late '90s and into the 2000s, the larger brewery was able to ship beer up to Bethel, allowing Mason to focus on more unique brews. In 2011, the brewery doubled the size of its system, moving up to a fourteen-barrel brewhouse.

THE BEER

With the **Sunday River Lager, Alt** and **Blonde** on regular rotation, Bethel's brewery stands out for having something different than the pale-brown-IPA-stout lineup of most brewpubs. Though none of the brews are flawless, all of Stoo's Brews are tasty and style-faithful beers.

Though Baxter Brewing Company has received a lot of press for its canning operations in Maine, I'll always remember **Sunsplash Golden Ale** as the first canned beer from the Pine Tree State. It's a shame the light, easy-drinking ale is no longer available in cans, but it's definitely worth a trip to the brewpub to pick up a growler during the hot summer months.

Sunday River also picked up the Stone Coast brands after the Portland brewery closed its doors in 2008. The best pieces of the defunct brewery's portfolio are its two India Pale Ales, the **420 IPA** and **840 IPA**. Both take the hop-forward American approach to IPAs rather than the more subtle English take, and the grapefruit citrus flavor of West Coast ales dominates. The bitterness of the hops comes forward in the 420, while the heavier malt base in the 840 (technically a double IPA) makes it the sweeter of the two beers. Stone Coast's **Jamaican Stout** is also noteworthy. Brewed in the style of a foreign export stout, the high-alcohol beer has serious bite and ends with a bitter coffee kick.

Sea Dog Brewing Company

26 Front Street, Bangor | (207) 947-8720
www.seadogbrewing.com | Founded 1993

THE BREWERY

I'm not sure if it's craftiness, creativity or just plain thriftiness, but Mainers have a habit of repurposing already-standing buildings to create their breweries. The state's brewing landscape is dotted with breweries and pubs in farmhouses, homes and old industrial structures. For Pete Camplin Sr., the ideal spot for his Maine coast brewery was a 128-year-old former woolen mill in Camden.

Camplin, a homebrewer by hobby and contractor by trade, saw a chance to combine his passions in the dilapidated mill. After an arduous rehab of the building that began in mid-1992 and ran through the next winter, Camplin had created a 240-seat brewpub and kegging brewery. The Sea Dog held its grand opening on May 17, 1993. The coastal brewery started with a fairly modest output, with production around 2,200 barrels a year by 1994. Still, between the success of the brewery with locals and the growing popularity of craft beer, Camplin saw room for expansion. After another property rehab (this time of a forty-five-year-old former shoe factory), Sea Dog Brewing Company opened a second location in Bangor. The larger 540-seat restaurant and brewery nearly quadrupled production, putting out 8,000 barrels of beer in 1995 and adding

The interior of Sea Dog's Bangor location, one of three it has in the state. *Photo courtesy of flickr user Cliff1066.*

bottled distribution to the Sea Dog portfolio. By the end of the decade, Sea Dog had added a pub in South Portland and Topsham.

When the craft beer bubble popped at the turn of the century, Sea Dog nearly sank with the industry ship. Facing debt and cash flow problems, the Sea Dog Brewing Company filed for Chapter 11 reorganization in November 2000. The company had completed its reorganization by September 2001, but problems continued and the company defaulted on its debt payments a year later. By the end of 2002, the company had filed for Chapter 7 bankruptcy. Luckily for the lovers of Sea Dog, Shipyard's Fred Forsley and Alan Pugsley—who were already contract brewing Sea Dog beer at their Portland brewery—swooped in to purchase the company.

Under the stewardship of Shipyard, the Sea Dog brand has recovered and flourished. Though the Camden brewpub has closed its doors, there are now three Sea Dog locations in Maine: Bangor, Topsham and South Portland. The brand has also spread south, with a Sea Dog brewpub in Clearwater, Florida (and another planned for Orlando), and "sister pubs" in three Massachusetts locations.

Sea Dog Brewing Company also fits into Maine brewing history as an incubator for a later generation of brewers. Kai Adams, a Maine native who had gone to college (and then on to brewing) in Colorado, was one of the brewmasters at Sea Dog's Camden location. Adams went on to found Sebago Brewing Company and eventually hired on Tom Abercrombie as the company's brewmaster. Abercrombie's start in brewing was as head brewer at Sea Dog, where he was originally hired by…Kai Adams.

THE BEER

When I think of Sea Dog's brews, the first thing that comes to mind is fruit beer. The Bangor brewery wasn't the first in the state to brew a blueberry ale (that distinction goes to Atlantic Brewing Company), but its **Blue Paw Wheat Ale** is undoubtedly the one most identified with Maine. Sea Dog has built on the fruit-and-wheat base, and it offers the **Apricot Wheat Ale** and **Raspberry Wheat Ale** in six-packs and on draft year-round. Sea Dog's take on fruit beers—light, sweet wheat ales that offer a stage for the fruit flavors—isn't my favorite, but there's no questioning the popularity of all three.

As with its parent company, Shipyard, most of Sea Dog's beers fit cleanly into a number of traditional English ale styles. The **Old East IPA**, **Old Golly Wobbler Brown Ale**, **Windjammer Blonde**, **Owls Head Light Ale**, **Pale Ale**, **Winter Ale** and **Sea Dog Stout** are all expertly crafted beers, if a bit on the safe side for some beer geeks.

A standout among Sea Dog's beers is the **Riverdriver Hazelnut Porter**. A traditional porter brewed with Willamette hops, four different malted barleys and a heavy dose of hazelnut, Riverdriver is a truly unique draft from the brewpub. The hazelnuts work well with the mix of malt, and the brew has won awards at a number of different beer fests such as the California Brewer's Festival and West Coast Brewer's Festival.

WHAT'S IN A NAME?

Sea Dog's name and logo both come from Barney, a Great Pyrenees owned by founded Pete Camplin. Despite the Pyrenees' legendary dislike of water, Barney took to the ocean with vigor. By spending about a quarter of the year on the decks of ships, he earned the distinction of Sea Dog, which carried over to the brewery where he acted as figurehead and "apprentice brewmaster."

Shipyard Brewing Company

86 Newbury Street, Portland | (207) 761-0807
www.shipyard.com | Founded 1994

THE BREWERY

Among all the breweries and brewpubs in Maine, Shipyard is the big momma. Alan Pugsley's brewhaus isn't just the biggest in Maine, though it easily passes that test at over eighty thousand barrels of beer a year. Shipyard's massive production scale positions it as the twenty-first-largest craft beer company in the United States, ahead of well-known brands like Rogue, Victory and Long Trail—all this from an Englishman with a love for Ringwood yeast.

Pugsley started brewing in the early '80s under the tutelage of Ringwood Brewery founder Peter Austin. When David Geary (of Geary's Brewing Company) needed some assistance launching his brewery, he contacted and contracted Pugsley, bringing the brewer to Maine. After the launch of Geary's, Pugsley stayed in the United States receiving and installing brewery equipment for aspiring stateside craft breweries. In the early '90s, Alan was back in Maine to help open Federal Jack's in Kennebunkport—a pub that doubled as a training facility for brewers. In 1994, Pugsley decided to put down roots and start a brewery of his own. With his business partner Fred Forsley, he opened Shipyard.

The exterior of Shipyard's massive Portland facility. *Photo courtesy of Shipyard.*

Buoyed by tax incentives from Portland, the pair chose a four-acre spot to house Shipyard. The massive facility, situated on Portland's waterfront in a former foundry building, holds the distinction of sitting on the birthplace of famed poet Henry Wadsworth Longfellow. It's a heritage the brewery chose to commemorate with its seasonal Longfellow Winter Ale.

Soon after beginning operations in 1994, the Shipyard Brewing Company made a move some in the industry saw as sacrilege. Facing debt and looking to finance expansion, half the brewery was sold to the behemoth Miller Brewing Company. In retrospect, it's hard to imagine that the deal could have worked more in the Maine brewer's favor. By 1996, Shipyard had tripled production from thirty thousand barrels to eighty-nine thousand. Miller's industry expertise and distribution network allowed Shipyard beers to disseminate around the country. Not only that, but the brewery soon returned to independence—Forsley and Pugsley bought Miller's shares back in 2000.

Back in the hands of the founders, Shipyard's runaway growth continued. By 2012, Shipyard Brewing Company was ranked as the sixteenth-largest craft beer company in the United States and shipped an astonishing 158,441 barrels of beer. With distribution in forty states and a number of countries, there's no doubt that the first Maine beer many drinkers try is one of Pugsley's brews.

While Shipyard's beers are a huge part of the Maine market in their own right, there are more beers brewed at its huge production facility than many beer drinkers may realize. On top of the Shipyard brand, the brewery acquired the Sea Dog, Carrabassett and Casco Bay brands in the last decade. Along with these three core brands, Shipyard contract brews beer for Gritty's, Davidson Brothers, Belfast Bay Brewing, the Woodstock Inn and Brewery, Hartford Better Beer, St. John Brewers and a few of the Atlantic Brewing brews. Peak Organic brews at Shipyard by way of an alternating proprietorship license. About 15 percent of the production at Shipyard is devoted to contract brews. Oh, and Captain Eli's sodas are all brewed at Shipyard as well.

THE BEER

Shipyard is an enthusiastic brewer of English-style ales—slavish, even. Its beers are all brewed with a proprietary Ringwood yeast strain, which gives them their distinctive house flavor. The notes that come from this particular type of yeast, mostly butterscotch and caramel, are divisive to say the least.

I'll put it right on front street—my palate just isn't built for the diacetyl levels that come from Ringwood beers, so a lot of Shipyard's beers (the **IPA** and **Export**, in particular) miss the mark for me. The maltier beers like the **Old Thumper** and **Blue Fin Stout**, however, benefit from the butterscotch and caramel flavors. And, of course, this is one man's opinion.

"We're not here to please everybody," noted Pugsley in an interview with beer writer Andy Crouch. "We're here to please the people who like our beers and we've got lots of them." As Maine's biggest brewery and one of the largest craft breweries in the country, it's obvious that Shipyard has far more fans than detractors.

In recent years, Shipyard brews have gained an inventive verve. The **Pugsley's Signature Series**, a series of high octane beers including a barleywine and imperial porter, put Pugsley's unique British spin on the world of "extreme" beer. Shipyard later introduced corked-and-caged, barrel-aged versions of some of these brews.

The newest addition to the brewery's regular lineup, the **Monkey Fist IPA**, shows the impact that West Coast craft brewers have had on the staid

Photo courtesy of Shipyard.

northeast. While it's still brewed with Shipyard's top-fermenting English yeast, the IPA is aggressively hopped with Warrior, Glacier and Cascade hops. The end result is a citrusy brew that strays further from traditional English ales than anything else in the Shipyard portfolio.

WHAT'S IN A NAME?

Shipyard's name comes from its neighborhood on Portland's waterfront, an area that traditionally housed shipbuilders, foundries and other manufacturers. The nautical theme extends to the Blue Fin Stout and the Monkey Fist IPA, which is named for a heavy knot used by sailors as both a weight and an occasional weapon.

Two of Shipyard's beers are named for famous Mainers. The Chamberlain Pale Ale is named for Joshua Chamberlain, former Maine governor and hero of the Battle of Gettysburg. Longfellow Winter Ale honors the poet Henry Wadsworth Longfellow, who happened to be born where the brewery now sits.

Allagash Brewing Company

50 Industrial Way, Portland | (207) 878-5385
http://www.allagash.com | Founded 1995

THE BREWERY

Ah, Allagash. While the Belgian-inspired brewery here in Portland isn't the biggest or highest-selling in the state, it has probably received the most critical acclaim. The flagship Allagash White—a wheat modeled after the popular Belgian witbier style—is one of the highest-rated wits brewed in the United States. Allagash White was the beer that founder Rob Tod first brewed back in 1995, when Allagash was a tiny one-man operation in the Turnpike Industrial Park.

Tod got his start in brewing at Vermont's Otter Creek Brewing, where he started out cleaning equipment and worked his way up to brewer. Having worked pretty much every job at a brewery, Rob was ready to set up shop in the beer-friendly Portland market. Construction began on Industrial Way in 1994, where Allagash was neighbored by craft brewers Geary's and the now-defunct Casco Bay. The fifteen-barrel brewery opened in July 1995, and Tod distributed kegs of his then draft-only Allagash White around Maine. It wasn't an immediate success—despite Maine's openness to craft beer, Mainers weren't yet used to the cloudy, spicy ales of Belgium.

Image courtesy of Allagash Brewing Company.

A sign inside Allagash's brewery that reflects the spirit and the culture of Tod's company. Image courtesy of Luiz Eduardo, flickr.

Eventually, drinkers wised up. Allagash White might not have been the beer locals were used to, but there was no question it was delicious. The beer quickly developed a cult following and still accounts for the vast majority of Allagash's sales.

In that first year of operation, Tod hired his first employee and introduced a second beer, a traditional Belgian dubbel called (fittingly) Allagash Dubbel. In 1998, Jason Perkins moved from working part time at Gritty McDuff's to a full-time position as Allagash's brewer. In the time since, Allagash has grown in size and stature. The brewery has undoubtedly been a trendsetter—Allagash was one of the first of what are now dozens of Belgian-style breweries in the states, and a move to cork-and-cage some of its line in 2001 has been copied by scores of brewers.

Allagash Black, aging in racks of barrels. *Image courtesy of Luiz Eduardo, flickr.*

In 2008, the brewery broke new ground once again, installing the first modern koelschip in the United States. The unique vessel is a shallow, fifteen-barrel steel pan used to cool down beer wort, which is simultaneously exposed to yeast floating in through the room's stained-glass windows. After a night of exposure to the open air, wort is pumped back into a fermentation tank for a year. After a year, it's pumped into oak barrels for even more aging. The result is a complex, dry, sour beer similar to traditional Belgian lambics. In 2010, Allagash began releasing small batches of koelschip beers to the public, four hundred 375-milliliter bottles at a time. These brewery-only releases continue to draw beer fans from all over and usually sell out in forty-eight hours or less.

In a far cry from that original fifteen-barrel system of the '90s, Allagash brewed over forty-five thousand barrels of beer in 2012. In 2013, Rob Tod expects to send over sixty thousand barrels of beer into the world. The number would match the brewery's stratospheric growth—since the mid-2000s, Allagash has increased production by 40 percent every year. In the fall of 2012, Allagash announced another expansion of 9,100 square feet, growing the brewhouse, retail store and the exterior fermentation tank structure. The expansion (the largest in the brewery's history) will increase production capacity around 45 percent. The expansion will also bring Allagash's staff to a little more than sixty people—a far cry from one guy handselling his quirky, cloudy Belgian beers.

The Beer

Allagash's flagship beer is **Allagash White**, a take on the traditional Belgian wheat beer. Brewed with loads of wheat and lightly spiced with coriander and orange peel, White has a crisp and spicy taste with a lingering fruity finish. The popularity of Allagash White is unrivaled in the brewer's catalog, with 75 percent of Allagash sales coming due to the brew. Maine isn't even the beer's biggest market—California is the country's largest buyer of White.

Keeping with the Belgian Trappist conventions that inspired the brewery, Allagash brews a **Dubbel** and a **Tripel**, along with a Quad (called **Four**). The year-round lineup is rounded out with a strong ale aged in bourbon barrels (**Curieux**) and the silky Belgian-style Stout **Allagash Black**.

Along with these year-round offerings, Allagash offers a "Tribute" series of four beers, proceeds from which go to different groups, organizations and funds. **Victoria** and **Victor**, ales brewed with Chardonnay and cabernet franc grapes respectively, benefit Portland landmarks the Victoria Mansion and the St. Lawrence Arts Center. The hoppy **Hugh Malone**, brewed with

Photo courtesy of Allagash.

60

a grain bill featuring Maine-grown barley, donates a dollar from every bottle sold to the Maine Organic Farmers and Gardeners Association. Finally, **Fluxus** is brewed to help fund a scholarship for Barbara Bush Children's Hospital pediatric nurses.

WHAT'S IN A NAME?

Allagash takes its name from the Allagash River and Allagash Waterway, a ninety-two-mile ribbon of lakes, streams and rivers in Northern Maine. The region gained its iconic status from Henry David Thoreau, whose journal from a trip on the river was a piece of *The Maine Woods*.

Hugh Malone and Victoria are named for two icons on different ends of the Portland compass. Hugh Malone, an Irishman and accomplished brewer, lived on Portland East End during the early 1900s. Hugh was a pioneer in the world of hopping ales, which explains why Hugh Malone is Allagash's hoppiest beer. Victoria is named for the Victoria Mansion, a distinguished architectural landmark of Portland's West End that was built in 1860. Victor's provenance is a bit less interesting—it's just a masculinized companion to Victoria.

Bray's Brewpub and Eatery

678 Roosevelt Trail, Naples | (207) 693-6806
www.braysbrewpub.com | Founded 1995

THE BREWERY

The building that holds Bray's is one of the oldest that I've covered in this book, but the brewery is a much more recent development. In 1995, Michael Bray and Michele Windsor moved to Maine and, despite a lack of any restaurant experience, wanted to open a brewery and pub. They settled on a 125-year-old inn in Naples, situated on the busy thoroughfare of State Route 302, to house the operation. The building already housed a restaurant, but the pair would make it their own and, more importantly, add a brewery to the attached barn.

Bray's wasn't the first tavern to occupy the space. Around the time of the American Revolution, an inn and tavern stood on the spot, serving folks traveling from Portland to the busy Sebago Lakes region. After a fire destroyed the building in the 1820s, it was rebuilt and sold. Ironically, the new owner was a temperance advocate, and the building went from drinking hole to temperance inn. Over the years it changed hands a few more times (and burned down once more) before being rebuilt as a Victorian farmhouse in 1880. By the time the Brays got their hands on the property, temperance and prohibition were distant memories, and alcohol could flow on the property once again.

Looking at Bray's from Route 302. The pub is on the right, and the brewery on the left. *Photo by the author.*

In August 1995, the restaurant operation passed to Michael and Michele, becoming Bray's. All it needed now was the "brew" part of the "brewpub and eatery." Michael was an avid homebrewer, but he needed to hustle to rig a large enough brewing system to house the brewery. The eventual 3.5-barrel system was put together from plenty of bits and pieces, including equipment that Michael "purchased" through trading his homebrews. The first Bray's beer was sold in December, just before the end of 1995.

The pub, squeezed into a 125-year-old Victorian farmhouse, probably has more character than all the bars in Portland put together. Given the building's former life as a home, it's of little surprise that Bray's is spread out among multiple rooms and multiple floors. If you're not one for a quirky layout, there's also an attached beer garden for beautiful Maine evenings—which offers a great space for the pub's nearly nightly musical guests.

If the beer isn't enough, the "eatery" part of the equation offers full pub, lunch and dinner menus, with Maine staples like lobster and shrimp joining sandwiches and pasta. Bray's is also well known for its beer dinners, which feature special menus, guest chefs and handpicked beer pairings from Michael.

Though it's kept its unique character over the years, a few changes have come to Bray's since 1995. For one, Michele and Michael no longer co-own the pub. The couple has split, and Michael now owns Bray's with his fiancée

Sonja LaRochelle. The other change is in the brewing department. Michael is no longer the "head brewer" at the pub—Rob Prindall has been Bray's brewmaster since '99.

The Beer

Kudos to Bray's brewmaster Rob Prindall, who hasn't stopped experimenting in the years he's been at the pub. A survey of its past and present brews reveals nearly thirty unique beers; a mix of one-offs, seasonal offerings, local favorites, classics and hybrid styles make up quite the rogue's gallery. If you'd like a chance to try everything Bray's brews, you've got one chance a year—in August, the pub's "One Night Stand" event changes all twenty-six taps over to different Bray's brews.

It'd be impossible to fit all of Bray's brews into this short section, but here's a look at some of the highlights.

My favorite amongst the pub's regular lineup is the **Causeway Cream Ale**. The uncommon style sits somewhere between ale and lager, brewed and fermented like an ale but with a lager yeast strain. The end result is a light-bodied beer with a sweet bread dough flavor and a creamy texture. A number of stellar IPAs are in regular rotation, including the **Mt Olympus Special Ale**, **Epicurean IPA**, **Zythonator** and a heavily hopped red ale cleverly termed **Redeye PA**. Prindall isn't scared to experiment with adjuncts to add color or flavor to his beers, and the **Viciously Vivacious Porter**, **Graveyard Stout** and **Yammityville Horror** respectively use vanilla, coffee and sweet potatoes.

If you fear the unknown or uncommon, don't worry. Bray's other regular offerings include a lighter blonde ale, a handful of pale ales, a brown and a couple porters.

What's in a Name?

When they opened Bray's Brewpub in 1995, Michele Windsor and Michael Bray were surprised to find that the pub shared a bit of etymological history with the town of Naples. Two of the town's founders were William Winsor and Washington Bray. With the shared last names and the fact that Michael was something of a "Washington" Bray himself (the couple had moved to Maine from the Evergreen State), the pair took the bit of history to be a good omen.

Many of Bray's beers are named for features of the brewery's backyard. The nearby Songo Lock, which links Long Lake and Brandy Pond with Sebago Lake, is honored with a Scotch Ale called Songo Loch. Causeway Cream Ale is named for the nearby causeway over the link between Long and Brandy. Pleasant Mountain Porter and Burnt Meadow Mountain Peated Porter both refer to nearby peaks.

Sheepscot Valley Brewing Company

74 Hollywood Boulevard, Whitefield | (207) 549-5330
www.sheepscotbrewing.com | Founded 1995

THE BREWERY

Steve Gorrill, better known as the "Count of Whitefield," is one of the more entertaining figures in Maine brewing. I mean, the fact that fans of his beer and Steve himself refer to the brewer as the "Count of Whitefield" is a bit of a red flag. The larger-than-life character fits in perfectly in Whitefield, a town packed with back-to-the-landers, artists and other creatives who flocked to Maine in the '70s.

Like a lot of Maine's brewers, Gorrill comes to professional brewing by way of homebrewing. After graduating from the University of Maine in 1985, Gorrill took up brewing as a way to try different styles of beer. He bounced around with his wife for a few years before settling in Maine as a shellfish farmer. At this point, he started exhibiting an entrepreneurial spirit shared with other Maine brewers—rather than work for someone else, Steve wanted to work for himself. In the interest of this (as well as spending more time with his wife and son), he started toying with the idea of starting a Whitefield brewery in 1994.

By that time, there were enough brewers in Maine that Gorrill had a few people he could reach out to for advice. Andy Hazen of Andrew's, Tod and

Suzi Foster of Bar Harbor and Kellon Thames and Dan McGovern of the (now defunct) Lake St. George Brewery all shared information about how they got their breweries off the ground. With this goodwill and good advice, the Sheepscot Valley Brewing Company was born in the summer of 1995. The unlikely location? The former Whitefield Cottage Hospital.

The brewery launched with a handful of Belgian ales, which were still a rarity in the states at that time. The Mad Goose Belgian-style ale, White Rabbit witbier and Moondance Bavarian-style Weiss were styles Gorrill loved but were difficult to sell in his part of Maine. Rather than truck the beer down to the more-hospitable Portland market, Steve switched gears. By 1997, he switched to more traditional British ales, and these brews proved a hit with locals. Less resilient was the brewery's short-lived mascot, "Joe Pemaquid." An anthropomorphized lobster buoy complete with a cigar and beer, Joe Pemaquid soon went the way of Joe Camel.

Sheepscot Valley Brewing continues to chug happily along, producing a few hundred barrels of beer a year. The brewery eventually moved from the former hospital to the barn at Steve's home on Whitefield's puzzlingly named Hollywood Boulevard. Sheepscot beer is available on draft at a few places in Portland—Three Dollar Dewey's and the Great Lost Bear were early supporters—but it's easiest to find in the brewery's neck of the woods. Plenty of local restaurants and bars tap kegs of the brewery's beer, and growlers are available at the brewery and in local stores.

Increased distribution doesn't seem to be in the cards at the moment. For years, Sebago brewed the flagship Pemaquid Ale in twenty-two-ounce bottles and in kegs, but Sebago's growth meant that by 2010 it didn't have any room on its equipment for non-Sebago beer. Staying small is just fine for the quixotic Gorrill—he'd much rather serve his local customers, spend time with his family and brew damn fine beer.

THE BEER

Currently, the brewery regularly brews four different beers; the easy-to-find **Pemaquid Ale** and **Boothbay Special Bitter**, and the spottier **Damariscotta Double Brown** and **New Harbor Lager**.

The Pemaquid Ale is Sheepscot's flagship brew. It's a malty, caramel-colored, dark amber brew, perfect either as a winter warmer or with seafood during the summer. The Double Brown is the closest the brewery has to anything "extreme," and at 7 percent ABV, it does pack more of a punch than most of the fare you pick up from Maine breweries. The Boothbay Special Bitter and Damariscotta Double Brown are both on the lighter end of the scale, good takes on the classic bitter and lager and great session brews.

Even though the four brews don't leave you with too many choices, boutique breweries have proven you might be better off doing one thing—and doing it well—than flooding the market with so-so beer.

Belfast Bay Brewing Company

100 Searsport Road, Belfast | (207) 338-2662
www.belfastbaybrewing.com | Founded 1996

THE BREWERY

The story of the Belfast Bay Brewing Company starts not with beer, but with ice cream.

John Patrick Mullen—or Pat, for short—is a native Mainer who, like so many, ended up transplanted in Massachusetts after college. Despite living and working out of state throughout the '60s, Pat and his wife (another native Mainer) traveled back to the Midcoast often. At the end of the decade, they decided to take up permanent residence in Maine. Soon after, they'd bought land on Belfast's Route 1, built a take-out joint and started selling Mullen's Old Fashioned Ice Cream. Pat was nuts about ice cream, y'see, and he started making the stuff five gallons at a time to sell to tourists. It proved so popular that there were soon Mullen's Ice Cream shops in Ellsworth and Bar Harbor.

It was in Bar Harbor that Mullen met Doug Maffucci, the brewer who would go on to found Atlantic Brewing and eventually own Bar Harbor Brewing Company. The two became friends over what one imagines were innumerable pints of beer and ice cream. When Patrick's restaurant—a property leased from Mullen—decided against renewing its lease in 1995, Mullen decided that the spot would be perfect for a brewery. He reached out to Maffucci, who helped him design the brewery and came on as a beer consultant for the new operation.

When he opened Belfast Bay Brewing Company in late 1996, Mullen made a smart move in hiring Dan McGovern as his head brewer. McGovern, who had owned the Lake St. George Brewing Company with Kellon James, had just closed up the Liberty brewery. Dan brought his brewing skill up the coast to Belfast, and the pair went on to brew nearly a dozen different Belfast Bay beers. Among the best was an oatmeal stout recipe similar to the one McGovern was best known for back in Liberty.

The attached pub (the Port Authority Brewpub) was designed by Mullen to be a showcase for Maine beer. Along with a dozen beers from Belfast Bay, the twenty-tap pub showcased only Maine breweries. The Port Authority also offered information and directions to other Maine breweries for guests who wished to visit them. It was a progressive move for a Maine beer bar, especially at a time when most other "local" breweries were at least an hour away.

Like Casco Bay, Sea Dog and Carrabassett, Belfast Bay is another Maine brewery that's been more or less swallowed up by the massive Shipyard Brewing Company. Mullen brought his two best brews—the Lobster Ale and McGovern's Oatmeal Stout—to Shipyard, and they're now mostly brewed and bottled in Portland. Mullen, a natural salesman, has transitioned from holding every role at Belfast Bay to simply marketing his beer. The shift in roles has undoubtedly helped Belfast Bay. With the help of Shipyard's distribution network, Mullen's beers are now available in over a dozen states and as far afield as Finland and Norway.

After the Belfast brewpub closed, both its equipment and brewer found a home nearby. Danny McGovern and Belfast Bay's seven-barrel brewing system both relocated to the Marshall Wharf Brewing Company, a popular brewery on the other side of the bay that was founded in 2007.

THE BEER

An oyster stout is brewed with oysters, and a milk stout contains lactose, but don't fret—Belfast Bay's flagship **Lobster Ale** doesn't contain an ounce of crustacean. Instead, it's a red ale with roasted malt, caramel and biscuit flavors. It's a slightly sweet but mild beer, and it pairs perfectly with a wide variety of foods.

McGovern's Oatmeal Stout, on the other hand, *is* brewed with oatmeal. The use of oats in the mash gives the final beer a silky smooth texture and a slightly creamy mouthfeel. It's a great year-round beer, light enough to enjoy during the summer but hearty enough to feel substantial during the winter.

WHAT'S IN A NAME?

Belfast's Lobster Ale was named after Maine's most famous seafood. Mullen's wife suggested—and rightfully so—that a Maine beer named Lobster Ale would be a surefire hit with locals and tourists alike.

Oak Pond Brewing

101 Oak Pond Road, Skowhegan | (207) 474-3233
www.oakpondbrewery.com | Founded 1996

THE BREWERY

While the Oak Pond brewery is in Skowhegan, Robert and Patricia Lawton weren't planning on opening a central Maine brewery when they founded the place. The beer's intended provenance was about one hundred miles away, at a bar in Portland called the Hedgehog Brewpub.

As young professionals in southern Maine (he a scientist, she a photographer), the Lawtons had dreams of one day opening a brewpub of their own. In fact, they went so far as to build a private pub—Snerben's—in their Gorham home. In the early '90s, they decided to take the leap and open a real brewpub in Portland. In 1995, the pair opened the Hedgehog Brewpub as a restaurant, only to find that zoning and licensing tied the prospect of brewing beer up in red tape. Robert had family in Skowhegan, so he had a novel idea: why not brew up in central Maine and just deliver the beer to the pub?

Lacking the initial start-up money for a brewery, the couple took the clever route of selling shares to their business partners to fund the venture. Family members were early investors, as were the carpenter and some of the brewery contractors. Chris Morton, Oak Pond's original brewer (and a transplant from Full Sail Brewing Company in Oregon), bought shares. Selling shares kept the price of the brewery down to about a third of what the Lawtons had initially worried. The whole affair was built in a former Skowhegan chicken barn, and a fifteen-barrel, five-hundred-gallon brewing system gave the brewery plenty of capacity to grow. Oak Pond shipped its first keg on July 18, 1996.

Over the next few years, Oak Pond supplied beer to the Hedgehog Pub and experimented with distribution locally and further abroad. Eventually, Hedgehog went under, and the operation went up for sale. By 2003, Oak Pond was set to close— and set to leave central Maine without a brewery of its own.

Don and Nancy Chandler bought the brewery from the Lawtons in 2003, soon after Don heard it planned to close. Don, who had a little experience homebrewing, apprenticed on the commercial system before taking over as head brewer when the sale went through. It's now fully a family affair, and the brewery operates seven days a week under the watch of Don, Nancy and their son Andy. Oak Pond self-distributes its beer, which is only readily available in about a fifty-mile radius of the brewery. A huge part of the brewery's sales come from growlers, perhaps because it offers one of the best deals in the state—eight dollars for a half-gallon of fresh, local beer.

I have fond memories of Oak Pond from the mid-2000s, when it was the beer provider for the Granary in Farmington, Maine. A former brewpub, the Granary decided to give up on brewing its own beer and instead kept five Oak Pond brews on as house beers. The Granary was the most popular bar in the town with college students, and there's no doubt that Oak Pond was an introduction to craft beer for many young Mainers.

Though the Granary has gone the way of the dodo, Oak Pond is still in the house beer business. The Chandlers brew three pale ales and a lager for the Boon Island Ale House in Wells.

THE BEER

Until the recent arrival of Bull Jagger Brewing in Portland, Oak Pond was the only brewery in Maine that focused primarily on lagers rather than ales. The majority of the brewery's beers—two year-round brews and both of its seasonals—are lagers. The devotion to lagers presents challenges; lagers require refrigeration to age and ferment correctly, and it's much harder to hide flaws and imperfections in a lager than an

Growlers account for a huge portion of Oak Pond's sales. At eight dollars for a fill, they're also among the least expensive craft beer in Maine. *Photo by DNA Photography.*

ale. However, Oak Pond proves that a focus on lagers can pay off with unique, flavorful beers.

For my money, the standout among Chandler's beers is the **Storyteller Doppelbock**. The winter seasonal, which needs to be cold conditioned for nearly three months before it's ready to drink, is an intensely strong brew. Heavy with flavors of nuts and toasted malt, it's a world-class take on a style that's been around for centuries. At 6 percent alcohol by volume, the beer has alcoholic strength to back up the intensity of flavor.

Oak Pod's other three lagers are, like the Storyteller, brewed in classic German styles. The summer seasonal **Laughing Loon Lager** is a Munich dunkel, and **Somerset Lager** is a German pilsner. The **Oktoberfest Lager** is crisp and bready, thankfully available in and out of the Oktoberfest season.

Like many other breweries in Maine and New England, Oak Pond brews a few ales that are quite similar to its English progenitors. The chocolate-tinged **Nut Brown Ale** and grassy **White Fox Ale** (an IPA) are mellow, drinkable beers. The **Dooryard Ale**, the brewery's flagship brew, is an American-style pale. Light and crisp with a kiss of wheat malt, it's not dissimilar from Baxter's Pamola Xtra Pale.

Kennebec River Brewery

1771 U.S. 201, The Forks | (800) 765-7238 |
www.northernoutdoors.com | Founded 1997

The Brewery

Given its rocky coast and verdant interior, it's unsurprising that Maine is home to a number of beautiful brewpubs and breweries. From Federal Jack's deck overlooking the Atlantic, to Bray's lakeside Victorian farmhouse, to Atlantic's estate brewery on Mount Desert Island, our state may be the prettiest place in the union to have a pint. Among this distinguished set of breweries, the Kennebec River Brewery takes the cake as the most scenic.

There's little question that most people driving up to The Forks are going for the spectacular whitewater rafting. In 1976, the Northern Outdoors Company—founded by Suzie and Wayne Hockmeyer—ran both the first rafting trip on the Kennebec River and the first rafting trip in the state of Maine. The timing, which coincided with the rise of whitewater rafting as a sport in the greater United States, couldn't have been better. By 1983, Northern Outdoors had built a lodge on 150 acres of pristine wooded land in northern Maine. The lodge also marked the transition of the company from a seasonal rafting outfit to a four-season resort that included snowmobiling, rock climbing, kayaking, camping and fishing.

Jim Yearwood, a raft guide who joined Northern Outdoors in 1981, developed a love of beer as the craft beer revolution began in the late '80s. In 1990, Jim started homebrewing. When the company began building improvements to its Resort Center and base of operations in the early 1990s, Yearwood suggested that an on-premises brewery would be a perfect addition. A combination of space for a production facility, a beer-loving staff and the clean, brewing-friendly water of the region gave the idea some legs. A 4.5-barrel brewing system imported from Canada replaced the resort's exercise room, and the Kennebec River Brewery released its first ale in January 1997.

Yearwood was head brewer for Kennebec River for the first few years of its existence and created the recipe for the brewery's flagship Kennebec River IPA. After a few years of brewing English-style ales, Jim transitioned into Northern Outdoors' senior management team (he's now vice-president). Mike McConnell, one of the founders of Rhode Island's Emerald Isle Brew Works, came on board as head brewer. A full-time guide, McConnell splits his time between brewing at the pub and guiding Northern Outdoors trips.

All of the beer brewed at the brewery is quite traditional—keg-conditioned, unfiltered and unpasteurized. Other than a handful of beers that are contract-brewed for distribution (originally by Casco Bay Brewing, and now by Mercury Brewing), you'll only find Kennebec River's beer at its pub on draft or in growlers. Though the brewery kegs its beer, it doesn't distribute it beyond its home base.

All said, it's definitely worth the trip to The Forks to try the beer. The Forks Resort Center, which houses both the brewery and the pub, is a classic open-timbered log lodge with a fieldstone fireplace, a twenty-four-person hot tub and unbeatable views of the surrounding wilderness.

THE BEER

If you stumble upon Kennebec River beer in the wild, you're likely to spot one of the three varieties contract-brewed by Mercury Brewing. The Massachusetts outfit brews Kennebec's year-round **Kennebec River IPA** and seasonals **Sled Head Red** and **Summer Ale** for distribution in bottles and six-packs. All three are solid takes on their respective styles, though not particularly exciting. The standout among these is the IPA, the first beer Kennebec brewed in '97 and arguably its flagship. Brewed with juicy Columbus, Summit and Magnum hops, the IPA is a citrusy treat with plenty of kick.

If you find Kennebec's beers at a brewfest or make it up to the brewery, you'll find a much deeper catalog of beers to choose from. Along with various one-offs and experiments, the Kennebec River Brewery has ten beers it brews at various times in the year. These range from varieties you'll find at other breweries around the state (a light lager, porter, stout and blueberry ale) to more unique fare. On the slightly quirkier side are the **Hazelnut Brown** and the **Honey Badger Rye**, a spicy-sweet rye ale brewed with honey and orange peel. McConnell also brews a German-style Schwarzbier, the suggestively named **Bear Naked Black Lager**.

Sebago Brewing Company

48 Sanford Drive, Gorham (production brewery) | (207) 856-2537
www.sebagobrewing.com | Founded 1998

The Brewery

Sebago Brewing Company is, in my mind, one of Maine's most underrated breweries. The quickly growing brewery tends to get lumped in with Maine's British-style brewers by locals and beer geeks, but Sebago is producing beers that fit snugly into the American brewing style. In fact, you won't find Fuggles or Maris Otter here—Sebago brews with all American ingredients. It may not be as on the cutting edge style-wise as Allagash or Marshall Wharf, but it is definitely brewing beers that (until recent years) have been hard to find from other Maine breweries. You could make a compelling argument that Sebago kicked off the "second wave" of American-style brewers that opened over the following decade in Maine.

Sebago Brewing was a joint effort from Kai Adams, Brad Monarch and Timothy Haines, who shared a common dream of opening a brewpub. Haines and Monarch were experts on the restaurant management end of things—Tim had run restaurants all over the country, and Brad had a degree in hotel and restaurant management. Adams was the beer guy. Kai had logged time at a brewhouse in Colorado as a University of Colorado–Boulder student, worked the bottling line at Geary's and was the first

Image courtesy of Sebago Brewing Company.

Sebago's production brewery in Gorham. The majority of the beer at the company's brewpubs is now actually produced here. *Photo by the author.*

head brewer at Sea Dog Brewing's ill-fated Camden location. With a business plan built from years of restaurant and brewpub experience, a Small Business Administration Loan, $75,000 from investors and some significant personal investments, the trio was ready to realize their dream.

Sebago opened the doors to its first location, a brewpub in South Portland, in 1998. Since then, expansion has been fast and furious. Now, the Sebago crew can count Kennebunk, Portland's Old Port and the village in Gorham as their homes as well. In 2005, the brewery opened a package facility and production brewery in Gorham, just a short distance from its brewpub. This moved most of the beer production outside of the Sebago restaurants, but it hasn't led to any drop in quality.

Sebago is one of Maine's largest brewing employers, with over 150 employees making up its restaurant, brewery and corporate team. It's not likely that number will shrink Adams has confessed an interest in opening more Sebago brewpubs both inside and outside of Maine.

The South Portland and Portland locations have seen changes in recent years, both moving to newer and more spacious locations. In his book *The Good Beer Guide to New England*, Andy Crouch notes that (at least initially) Sebago was better known for food at its pubs than beer. While the beer now gets a bit more attention, the menus at each restaurant are still worthy of high praise. You won't find a better plate of potato nachos anywhere.

THE BEER

In recent years, Sebago's lineup of beers has ballooned from a handful of year-round and seasonal beers to a deep catalog of interesting brews. With five seasonals, five year-round brews and a highly anticipated "Single Batch" line, there's nothing in Sebago's lineup that disappoints.

Sebago's year-round line is full of brewpub classics. The **Frye's Leap IPA** is one of Maine's best, brewed with loads of American hops and further dry-hopped to the tune of a pound of hops per barrel. A backbone of sweet caramel malt balances out the intense fruitiness of the hop bill. The **Runabout Red**, **Boathouse Brown** and **Lake Trout Stout** admirably fill out the rest of Sebago's beer spectrum. The brewery also has one of the state's better light beers in **Saddleback Ale**, a crisp brew in the style of a Czech lager.

Sebago's seasonals kick off the year with the **Full Throttle Double IPA**, available from February to April. It's a bitter hop bomb that would fit right in among the imperial IPAs of the West Coast. It's followed up by a **Hefeweizen** that's a bit bolder than many takes on the style, with beautiful banana and clove flavors (be sure to order it without lemon). Summer also sees **Bass Ackwards Berryblue Ale**, a mild ale brewed with so much blueberry that it takes on a purple hue. Fall's **Local Harvest Ale** lives up to its name, brewed with locavore-friendly Maine hops, barley and water. The production is even hyper-local, with the hops harvested by Sebago fans, friends and staff at a hop-picking party. The year closes out with the winter warmer **Slick Nick Winter Ale**, a malty strong ale available during the coldest months of the year. Like Gritty McDuff's, Sebago is one of the few breweries in Maine that brews a winter ale without any spices added—a welcome decision.

Recent years have seen an expansion of both pilot beer nights (draft-only events featuring brews from Sebago staffers) and single batch beers available in twenty-two-ounce bottles. My favorite so far has been the **Grand Crüe**, an annual bottled release of blends of multiple Sebago brews.

Freeport Brewing Company

110 Breakwater Drive, South Portland | (207) 767-2577
No Website Available | Founded 1999

THE BREWERY

In 1999, Ken Collings and Michael Olinsky started one of the nation's smallest nanobreweries in Freeport, Maine. Originally constructed from a secondhand brewing system built in Olinsky's repurposed barn, Freeport Brewing Company had a maximum output of one hundred barrels a year. It was certainly Maine's smallest brewery when it was founded, and its production was somewhere south of one-tenth of one percent of what a giant like Shipyard produces.

At the time of its founding, Freeport self-distributed its beer to just a handful of accounts—kegs to the Broad Arrow Tavern and Jameson's in Freeport and the Great Lost Bear in Portland and twenty-two-ounce bottles to beer stores in a roughly ten-mile radius. Michael left the brewery a few years in, leaving Ken as the sole brewer, distributor, owner and everything else of Freeport Brewing Company. In early 2010, production proved to be high enough that Collings brought on Shaina Laroche as assistant brewer.

After a decade of brewing, FBC nearly joined the ranks of Maine's many defunct breweries. In mid-2010, the building that housed the brewery was sold, and Collings had to put his brewing on hold and his

Image courtesy of Freeport Brewing Company.

equipment into storage. Though the brewer remained upbeat that he'd find a new home (either in Freeport or elsewhere), I was one of many local beer fans holding my breath.

In 2012, Collings found a new home for his two-barrel system. One big difference this time around is that Freeport Brewing Company is no longer in Freeport. Collings set up his brewery on South Portland's Breakwater Drive, just a few dozen miles south of his original farmhouse brewery. The relaunch was led by Freeport's Blonde Ale, which appeared on tap at a few restaurants in Freeport. Now that the brewery is a bit more established in SoPo, you can find Ken's beer in growlers and on draft all over Southern Maine.

THE BEER

During its years in Freeport, the Freeport Brewing Company had a substantial mix of brews available around Southern Maine. Since reopening in South Portland, Collings has slowly been scaling his way back up one recipe at a time. Thankfully, he's started with some of his best beers (and they, thankfully, aren't adversely affected by the South Portland water).

Brown Hound Brown Ale, Freeport's flagship brew, is a stellar example of the style. With coffee and chocolate notes and the slightest kiss of hops, the brown is easily sessionable and a perfect pair to food. The **Ex-Wife**

Bitter Blonde offers a lighter shade of ale. It's a crisp, toasty blonde with a surprisingly aggressive hop bite.

The **Chocolate Porter** is Ken's best beer. It's a mild porter, amped up with delicious bittersweet chocolate flavors. It's light enough to be easy to drink, but full-bodied enough to be completely satisfying.

The Liberal Cup Public House and Brewery

115 Water Street, Hallowell | (207) 623-2739
www.theliberalcup.com | Founded 2000

THE BREWERY

Now celebrating more than a decade of life on Hallowell's waterfront, the Liberal Cup is an institution in the central Maine beer scene. It's the product of Geoff Houghton's longstanding love of the British pub culture, as well as a good number of years spent in the beer business on both sides of the Atlantic.

After spending time in England as a teenager and then again as a young adult, Houghton decided that pub ownership would be his ideal career path. As he grew older, he decided that brewing would also be a pretty nice gig. Without many brewery jobs presenting themselves in the United States in the '80s—this was, after all, just the earliest days of the craft brewing movement—Houghton worked as a brewer at Ian Hornsey and Dick Burge's newly opened Nethergate Brewery in England. The brewery, with a focus on traditional bitters and cask ales, provided plenty of inspiration for the beer that Houghton would eventually brew at the Liberal Cup.

Before opening his own brewpub, Houghton worked with a few of Maine's early masters. After leaving Nethergate in 1989, Geoff spent time in the breweries at both Gritty McDuff's and D.L. Geary's. Life got in the way of his opening a brewpub of his own, but by 2000, time and fate aligned enough for Houghton to open the Liberal Cup in Hallowell.

Owner and brewmaster Geoff Houghton opened the Cup in order to get his personal brews out to the masses and added food to the menu "as a catalyst to get people to come in and drink the beer." Eventually the pub became as well known for its food as its beer. It's a testament to the food, considering the quality of Houghton's beers.

The food is about what you'd expect from a Brit-inspired pub, with a good amount of Maine coasty stuff thrown in. Big portions, hearty food and stick-to-your-ribs fare for the frequently chilly weather in Maine are all par for the course (I'd recommend the meatloaf sandwich). The atmosphere is warm and friendly, the staff is kind and attentive and a heavy schedule of musical guests, trivia nights and other events keeps the place busier than you might expect for a bar in Hallowell.

In 2008, Geoff opened a second brewpub in southern Maine. The Run of the Mill, affectionately referred to by Houghton as "Liberal Cup South," was opened on Saco Island in a space nearly twice the size of the Liberal Cup. Equipment from the defunct Sugarloaf Brewing Company was installed in the pub; while the sister enterprises share many recipes, the pubs both brew their own beer.

Along with helping to build a craft beer culture in central Maine, one of Houghton's biggest impacts on Maine beer was his push for LD 904, a

Renovations early in 2012 modernized the pub, bringing in much-appreciated touches like a redone brewhouse and a new bar top. *Photo courtesy of the Liberal Cup.*

change in Maine statute that allowed brewpubs to sell half-gallon "growlers" of beer from their taps for consumers to take home. Houghton was the inspiration for the law, which was spearheaded by Representative Nancy Smith and passed in 2009. LD 904 has revolutionized the Maine beer landscape. Brewpubs and draft-only breweries like Geaghan's, Oxbow and Bunker Brewing have had huge success with growlers. The Liberal Cup and Run of the Mill both sell unique growlers for thirsty publicans to take home.

In early 2012, the Liberal Cup went through some significant renovations, seriously rehabbing the decade-old restaurant. Despite the changes, the Cup maintained the dark wood, low lights and communal charm of an English pub. Straddling the line between English and American cultures, it fits perfectly on the quaint Main Street of Hallowell.

THE BEER

In a state already heavy with ales inspired by the brewpubs of the United Kingdom, the twenty-one brews from the Liberal Cup still stand out as some of the best British brews in Maine. Throughout the year, Houghton and crew brew some twenty-one different beers, and the bar always has about a half-dozen different choices on tap. In the British tradition, one of these is always of the cask-conditioned variety.

In the classic British school, the Cup brews a stout, a porter and three different bitters. Slightly off the beaten path are the **Tarbox Cream Stout** and **Chazmo Altbier.** The former is a stout sweetened with lactose, and the latter is a German Altbier—a style brewed by many in New England but few in Maine. Another fairly unique offering is the **Bug Zapper "Super" Lager**, a malty red lager that looks much more like an ale at first glance.

All the beers from the Liberal Cup are great, but I'd highly recommend the cask **Bitter** or **Oatmeal Stout** if you're looking for the best of the best. Or get a flight of all that they have on tap.

WHAT'S IN A NAME?

All of the brewpub's ales are served in imperial twenty-ounce pints—a fact that Houghton states at least partially in the restaurant's name. Certainly, I can imagine my disappointment if I went to a place called the Liberal Cup and got a Conservative Pour.

Marshall Wharf Brewing Company

2 Pinchy Lane, Belfast | (207) 338-1707
www.marshallwharf.com | Founded 2007

The Brewery

When they opened Belfast's 3Tides bar and restaurant in 2003, David and Sarah Carlson were determined to bring something unique to the Maine Midcoast. A martini and tapas bar, while workable in trendy Portland, may have been a tough sell for the sleepy town of Belfast. To my delight and that of other Maine beer-lovers, the idea not only flourished but also gave birth to one of the state's best breweries.

In the early 2000s, David and Sarah moved to Maine from Wyoming, hoping to build their dream bar. They were both native Mainers, and like so many of the state's brewery proprietors, they felt the magnetic pull of the Pine Tree State and needed to return home. For a location, they settled on two old buildings on the Belfast waterfront, including the town's original granary. The interior and exterior of 3Tides were (and still are) a bit of a mish-mash—lampshades, wood, corrugated aluminum and poured concrete.

Down East Magazine asked why Carlson thought such a venture would work in Belfast.

Carlson gave a simple answer: "Because it didn't exist," he says. "There are enough smart collective individuals from every walk of life that if

Image courtesy of Marshall Wharf Brewing Company.

something is not here, people will come up with it, create it, and it will be accepted. That's the attitude I love."

Since 2003, the complex has grown to include two levels, two bars, an outdoor fireplace and the bocce court that seems to be so in vogue with beer lovers. In 2007, the Carlsons made the major addition of a seven-barrel in-house brewery next door, to be named the Marshall Wharf Brewing Company.

When seeking a head brewer, Marshall Wharf brought in one of Maine's best. Over the years David had struck up a friendship with Danny McGovern, a masterful brewer who had co-founded the Lake St. George Brewing Company and then brewed for Belfast Bay. McGovern came on board as Marshall Wharf's brewmaster. Though Danny had made some unique beers for his brewery and Belfast Bay, they come off as downright restrained compared to the quirky brews he's crafted at his new home.

Marshall Wharf, self-described as the "bad boys" of Maine brewing (blame it on the high-alcohol, experimental, hard-to-find beers), could be considered the forefathers of the second wave of craft brewing in Maine. It wasn't the first Maine brewery to reject English ale styles and yeast like Ringwood and Nottingham—Allagash and Sebago both did that about a decade earlier—but it went the farthest afield from traditional beer styles. There's no question that the high-octane beers of Marshall Wharf have had a massive influence on the breweries that have opened in Maine since 2007.

After years of only putting its beer out on draft or in growlers, Marshall Wharf took the leap into canning its beer for distribution in 2012. The brewery has taken the interesting tack of using generic Marshall Wharf cans with the beer name, alcohol content and a UPC code attached via an adhesive

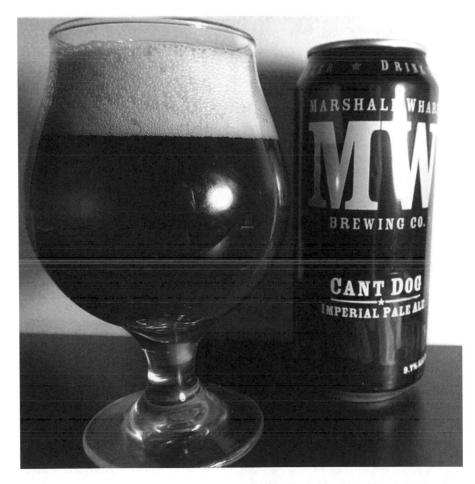

The introduction of cans in 2012 made Marshall Wharf's ales much easier to bring home. The brewery discussed a number of different brews for its inaugural cans, but eventually decided on its heavily hopped Cant Dog. *Photo by the author.*

label. That means that, rather than commit to massive quantities of a single beer in a beer-specific can, Marshall Wharf has the opportunity to rotate through a number of its brews. Carlson and McGovern have committed to a two-hundred-gallon batch of beer each week to be canned. The move doesn't mean that the brewery's wares will be available everywhere—it does still self-distribute its beer—but it does mean fans can take home Marshall Wharf beer without a drive up to Belfast.

THE BEER

The selection of beer available from Marshall Wharf is simply staggering. With over thirty different beers in its portfolio and seventeen MW taps at the attached 3Tides, it's likely you have more options at one time from Marshall Wharf than any other Maine brewery.

If you can't make it up to the Belfast brewery, the beer you're most likely to find on draft or in cans is the immensely popular **Cant Dog Imperial IPA**. It was born out of a bit of luck—Marshall Wharf managed to get a deal on loads of Simcoe hops (a pine-like bittering hop with notes of citrus) from a down-on-his-luck Idaho brewer. The end result is an amber-colored hop bomb, a tongue-coating IPA rich with the flavors of orange, pine and grapefruit. It also hides its alcohol better than any other 10 percent ABV beer I've had. Be careful if you're drinking these.

Marshall Wharf's other brews run the gamut from sessionable fare like the lightweight **Pinchy Red Ale** and **Little Moo Brown Ale** to the robust **Chaos Chaos Russian Imperial Stout** and **T2-R9 Barleywine**. Marshall Wharf's beers draw inspiration from all over the globe, from Britain (**Pemaquid Oyster Stout, Sea Level Stout, Cornholio Welsh Blonde Ale**) to Germany (**Wiener German-style Vienna Lager, Attenuator Doppelbock, Docktor Dunklesweizen**), to Belgium (the tart **Bitty** and peppery **Spicy Ace Hole**).

Brewer Dan McGovern makes the most of his recipes, and a number of Marshall Wharf's beers are alternate takes on a single recipe or "small" beers brewed from the same grains as the stronger ales. Little Mayhem, Little Max and Little Toot are weaker "little brothers" to Chaos Chaos, T2-R9 and the **Maximillian Imperial Red Ale**. **Sexy Chaos** is a variation on Chaos Chaos aged on vanilla beans and oak chips, and **Scott's Scoville Chili Ale-Ien** combines the **Illegal Ale-Ien** kolsch/wheat hybrid with jalapeno and habanero peppers.

Peak Organic Brewing

110 Marginal Way, #802, Portland | (207) 586-5586
www.peakorganic.com | Founded 2005

THE BREWERY

In the early 2000s, a young Jon Cadoux and his friends were avid homebrewers looking to go pro. Cadoux had begun incorporating organic ingredients into his beer—no small feat, since organic barley and hops weren't necessarily easy for homebrewers to find. He cleverly built relationships with organic farms and co-ops, bootstrapping his way to all-natural beer ingredients. With rave beer reviews from local friends and the entrepreneurial bona fide of an MBA from Harvard, Jon took the leap into commercial brewing in 2005. Geoff Masland was on board as Peak's sales and marketing manager. Masland would go on to found Newcastle's Oxbow Brewing with brewer Tim Adams.

Peak Organic certainly picked the right time to enter the market: organic beer has become a fast-growing part of the beer business and one of the fastest growing segments of organic food. In 2003, organic beer sales totaled about $9 million. That number had jumped to $19 million by the time Peak was founded in 2005 and over $41 million in "green" brew by 2010.

USDA standards for organic certification are pretty strict: at least 95 percent of the ingredients in a product must be organically grown (which means no chemical pesticides and no chemical agents), and none of the ingredients can

Image courtesy of Peak Organic.

be chemically engineered. As an early entry into the organic brewing arena and an all-organic brewery, Peak has been supportive of the strict standards. Cadoux is an enthusiastic locovore and environmentalist, and green beer isn't a gimmick but a passion. However, the devotion to organic ingredients isn't at the expense of quality. As the brewer told the *Wisconsin Beer Geek* blog in a 2012 interview, "We refuse to buy an ingredient just because it's organic, it has to be excellent first and organic second to make it in the door. We strive to produce beer that is extremely exceptional, as well as organic."

Rather than build a production brewery for Peak Organic, Jon and his team opted to brew on someone else's equipment. By way of an alternating proprietorship license, the brewery crafts its beer at Portland's Shipyard Brewing Company. As of 2012, Peak was producing more than fifteen thousand barrels of organic beer for thirsty drinkers on both coasts of the United States.

THE BEER

Though the organic ingredients distinguish Peak Organic from the other brewers in Maine, the brewery's regular line-up features styles typical of the region. With the **Peak IPA**, **Amber Ale**, **Nut Brown** and **Pale Ale**, the brewery offers a nice mix of malty and hoppy beers. The IPA is the standout of the bunch. Hopped with Simcoe, Amarillo and Nugget hops for flavor and aroma, but lacking any bittering hops, the IPA offers the taste of hops without much accompanying bitterness.

Peak's seasonal rotation is one of my favorites in Maine. Each season, the brewery puts the focus of its quarterly beer on a single hop. In the **Simcoe Spring**, the brew is single-hopped and dry-hopped with Simcoe, giving it strong notes of fruit and pine. The **Summer Session**, a crisp wheat ale brewed with locally grown wheat, puts Amarillo hops on center stage. **Fall Summit** features Summit hops and is brewed with toasted malts and fermented cold for a dry, biting finish. The dark, wheat **Winter Session** is single-hopped and dry-hopped with Citra hops. The unique hop is known for pineapple flavors, which are a pleasant contrast to the spicy, earthy wheat.

Along with the seasonals and standard lineup, Peak offers a creative mix of special brews. A couple are collaborative efforts, which fits nicely with the brewery's local, organic ethos. The **Espresso Amber** is brewed with organic espresso from Portland coffee roasters Coffee by Design. It makes for a unique beer—most coffee ales are stouts or porters, and the toffee flavor of the Munich malt plays against the roast of espresso. The **Maple Collaboration** combines Peak Organic's beer with organic oats from Maine's GrandyOats (giving it a smooth body) and maple syrup from Butternut Mountain Farms (providing a sweet finish).

Finally, the brewery's **Local Series** explores how local terroir affects a beer. Four beers have been brewed in the series, each following the same base recipe but made with hops and barley from a particular state. The beers showcase the local flavors of Maine, Vermont, Massachusetts and New York.

The Black Bear Brewery

9 Mill Street, Suite 4, Orono | (207) 949-2880
www.blackbearmicrobrew.com | Founded 2008

THE BREWERY

To tell the history of the Black Bear Brewery, you first have to back up and look at the Bear Brew Pub. It's something you can literally do, since the two businesses are neighbors.

The Bear Brew Pub, opened by Yugoslavian immigrant Milos Blagojevic in 1995, was Orono's original craft brewery. A cozy, dark-wood restaurant with a beer garden out front, the place was a bit of a mix of college bar and classic New England brewpub. The centerpiece of the operation was a small brewing system where Milos brewed an assortment of unfiltered ales.

In the late '90s, University of Maine student Tim Gallon and his friend Matt Haskell started working for Milos at the pub. Milos trained Gallon—already a homebrewer—on the ins and outs of commercial brewing. When Blagojevic was ready to leave the brewing business in 2002, Gallon and Haskell jumped on the opportunity to buy him out. Haskell ran the business, and Gallon found himself promoted from apprentice to head brewer. Though he never took any professional brewing courses, Tim built a brewing knowledge base through beer books, websites, chatting with other brewers and, of course, lots of hands-on experience.

SAID PROHIBITION MAINE TO PROHIBITION GEORGIA:
"Here's Looking At You."

Above: *Photo by the author.*

Left: This cartoon from *Puck* magazine shows how ineffective the Maine Law and its like were in preventing drinking. Captioned: "Said prohibition Maine to prohibition Georgia: 'Here's looking at you,'" the image shows a Mainer and a Georgian hoarding Cold Tea and Orange Phosphate, two regionally popular alcoholic beverages. *Courtesy of the Library of Congress, LC-DIG-ppmsca-26196.*

Above: Gritty's
Black Fly Stout,
with a scoop
holding hops
visible in the
background.
*Photo courtesy of
Gritty McDuff's.*

Left: *Photo by the
author.*

Bass Harbor Head Light, the namesake for Harbor Lighthouse Ale, marks the entrance to Bass Harbor and Blue Hill Bay. *Photo by Guillén Pérez.*

Given the brewpub's proximity to the Sunday River ski resort, it's unsurprising that the sample flights are served on repurposed skis. *Photo courtesy of Russell Sprague, flickr.*

www.seadogbrewing.com

Image courtesy of Sea Dog Brewing Company.

One of Sea Dog's most popular beers is its blueberry-infused Blue Paw ale. *Photo courtesy of flickr user Tony Fischer.*

Opposite, top: Image courtesy of Shipyard Brewing Company.

Image courtesy of Belfast Bay Brewing Company.

Image courtesy of Kennebec River Brewery.

A brew in progress on KRB's system. Fermenters are visible in the background. *Photo courtesy of Kennebec River Brewing Company.*

Above: Though the Kennebec River Brewing Company bottles a handful of its beers, the only way to get most of the company's ales and lagers is to fill a growler at the brewery. *Photo courtesy of Kennebec River Brewing Company.*

Right: For years, the only way to bring home beer from Marshall Wharf was to fill a growler at its brewery in Belfast. *Photo courtesy of Jake Christie.*

Photo by the author.

Run of the Mill's unique growlers. *Photo by the author.*

Previous, top: Image courtesy of Baxter Brewing.

Previous, bottom: The move to Fox Street in 2012 allowed Rising Tide to increase the size of its brewing setup substantially. *Photo courtesy of Rising Tide Brewing.*

Right: Brewer Nathan Sanborn surveys Rising Tide's growing barrel aging program. *Photo courtesy of Rising Tide Brewing.*

Below: Photo by author.

Portland's Stone Coast Brewing closed in 2008. *Photo courtesy of flickr user Cliff1066.*

The Kennebunkport Brewing Company at Federal Jack's. *Photo by the author.*

Previous, top: An early bottle from Portland's Maine Mead Works. *Photo by the author.*

Previous, bottom: Cold River Vodka, a 100 percent Maine potato vodka. *Photo courtesy of Maine Distilleries LLC.*

The front of the Great Lost Bear, "Maine's Microbrew Tap House." *Photo courtesy of flickr user Bernt Rostad.*

The extensive tap list at the Lion's Pride, above its unique blown-glass tap handles. *Photo by the author.*

Right: Mama's Crowbar. *Photo by the author.*

Below: Win and Lori Mitchell, founders of the Boothbay Craft Brewery. *Photo by the author.*

Left: The interior of Oxbow's Newcastle brewhouse. *Photo courtesy of Michael Donk, brewbokeh.com.*

Below: Photo courtesy of Gritty McDuff's.

Despite the popularity of the pub's beers, Gallon decided he needed more space than the 500 square feet at Bear to establish a full-scale brewing operation. In 2007, Tim sold Matt his share of the pub and purchased a 2,500-square-foot shop across the street. Thus, the Black Bear Microbrewery was born. A ten-barrel brewhouse was installed that year, and Gallon sold his first beer in 2008.

At the time of this writing, the brewery is composed of a ten-barrel brewing system and a handful of ten- and twenty-barrel fermenters. Black Bear is a two-man operation, with Gallon and assistant brewer Matt York able to crank through a couple large batches a day. Being a draft-only brewery frees the pair up from a bottling line, but cleaning and filling kegs—along with all the other business of running a full-size brewery—keeps the tiny staff busy. Rather than self-distribute, Black Bear distributes beer through Penobscot, Aroostook, Hancock, Washington and Piscataquis counties via Maine Distributors. It makes them one of the state's only breweries (along with Oak

Pond in Skowhegan) that's easy to find in Central and Eastern Maine but nearly impossible to find in the brewvana of the Portland area.

The newest addition to Black Bear is a taproom, which opened in the summer of 2012 and allows visitors to sample brews by the paddle or pint. The cozy taproom, which houses a six-seat bar and a few tables, also acts as the brewery's growler-filling station. Thanks to changes in Maine law in 2011 that allowed breweries to sell beer for on-site consumption without selling food, similar additions are being done at a number of other Maine breweries like Oxbow and Maine Beer Company.

Tim Gallon, Black Bear founder and brewmaster.
Photo courtesy of Chad Lothian.

THE BEER

Through years of brewing with Milos Blagojevic—and then on his own—at the Bear Brew Pub, Gallon developed a keen taste for what his local customers prefer in their beer. With his new brewery, larger and separate from the pub, he's been able to hone his most popular recipes while experimenting with new, different brews.

Black Bear's two most popular ales are undoubtedly **Gearhead Ale** and **Pail Ale**. Gearhead, an amber hopped with English hops, walks a tightrope between British and American beer styles. Roasted barley and chocolate malt add some surprising complexity to the amber brew. The Pail Ale is a well-done take on the typical craft brewery pale ale, hopped aggressively with Cenntenial and Cascade hops for a grapefruit nose and flavor.

Gallon also brews two different types of IPA, a style that's always popular with craft beer drinkers. The **Tough End IPA** is a hoppy West Coast–style India Pale Ale, and its massive citrus notes make it seem like a big brother to the Pail Ale. The other IPA, **Bad Omen**, is one of the few Black IPAs brewed in Maine. The style, which is growing in popularity around the country, combines the aggressive hopping of American IPAs with darker malts, which balance the floral flavors with a roasted kick.

The Black Bear Microbrewery brews winter and summer seasonals (which are likely to appear right around finals week at the nearby University of Maine, to the delight of students). Winter brings the dark and robust **Tree Tugger Barley Wine** and **Voodoo Porter**, while summer calls for the **Liquid Sunshine** hefeweizen and another inescapable Maine **Blueberry Ale**.

Run of the Mill Public House

100 Main Street, Saco | (207) 571-9652
www.therunofthemill.net | Founded 2008

THE BREWERY

Geoff Houghton knows how to run a damn fine brewpub. One need look
no further than the Liberal Cup in Hallowell (Geoff's first place, opened
in 2000) to see the great food, beer and atmosphere that a well-run public
house can produce. Geoff replicated his success at the Liberal Cup's sister
pub, the Run of the Mill Public House and Brewery in Saco.

In early 2008, rumors were swirling around Maine that there was a
new brewpub coming to Saco. The rumored "Brick Island Brewing" was
to be the first commercial entity on Saco Island, taking up residence in a
former textile mill. That March, the *Kennebec Journal* broke the news that
Run of the Mill (affectionately known as "Liberal Cup South") would be
open by summer.

Houghton, the managing partner in the new pub, teamed up with attorney
Severin Beliveau and developer Kevin Mattson to make the Run of the Mill
a reality. Both Beliveau and Mattson were part of Island Point Development,
a real estate developer revitalizing the entirety of Saco Island. The massive
thirteen-thousand-square-foot brewery and pub was just the first part of a
major rehabilitation of the four factory buildings on the island.

The brewpub boasts a few connections to Maine's rich brewing history. As a brewmaster, Houghton scored Nate Duston, who formerly brewed for Casco Bay Brewery in Portland (as well as Oregon's Bridgeport Brewing). The Run of the Mill's fourteen-barrel brew system came from Sugarloaf Brewing Company, which had quit the on-site brewing business years earlier. The connection to the Liberal Cup also runs deeper than simply ownership—a number of the items on the Saco pub's food and beer menu are borrowed from its sister operation.

With seating for nearly two hundred people—and more room on a massive deck overlooking the Saco River—Run of the Mill is easily one of Maine's largest brewpubs. As great as the public house's beer is (and, believe me, Duston can brew), it definitely comes across as a pub first and a brewery second. The menu is packed with delicious British-style food like shepherd's pie and bangers and mash, along with sandwiches, wraps and soups. The spacious deck, open during the summer, adds a grill menu and raw bar. A busy event schedule includes Monday night trivia and live music on Tuesdays, Thursdays and Saturdays. Of particular note is a yearly Brewer's Dinner, a six-course meal with specially designed and paired brews and food.

Like many of Maine's pubs, Run of the Mill offers growlers so publicans can take their beer home. The ornate twenty-five-dollar growlers are perhaps the most impressive I've ever seen. Offered in a rainbow assortment of colors, the lantern-shaped, swing-top growlers are works of art whether full or empty.

THE BEER

Like its sister brewery the Liberal Cup, the focus at Run of the Mill is on classic British styles. In fact, a number of the available beers are the same ones that are offered up in Hallowell. Along with the shared brews, Duston brews a good number of beers that only appear in Saco.

Some of the brews, like the **Impact Pale Ale** and **What's Hoppenin' XPA**—an IPA and double IPA—have a distinctly American bent. Others draw inspiration from around the world, from the German **Mudflap Spring Bock** and **Dunkel John's Band** to the Scottish **Tented Kilt Scottish Ale**.

At a burly 7-plus percent alcohol, the winter seasonal **Smelt Camp Strong Ale** is among the strongest beers offered by Run of the Mill. The ESB has the same balance and hits the same flavor notes as the flagship **Alewife Ale**, but the strength basically makes it that beer's big brother.

WHAT'S IN A NAME?

The many historical mills and factories of Saco Island give the brewery its name. Since the 1600s, the island has housed sawmills, iron works, manufacturing plants, cotton mills, a tannery and a Nike shoe factory (among other businesses). The Run of the Mill sits in old Building #3, which was built in 1838.

Maine Beer Company

525 U.S. Route 1, Freeport | (207) 221-5711
www.mainebeercompany.com | Founded 2009

THE BREWERY

Maine Beer Company began its life as a small brewery (Nanobrewery? Picobrewery?) located on Portland's Industrial Way. Started in 2009 by two homebrewing brothers, Maine Beer began on a single-barrel brewing system, barely more than a homebrew kit. While the family brewery has grown substantially in the few years it's been around, the founding pair's devotion to putting the beer first and foremost has paid off.

A few years ago, Daniel and David Kleban—from away, but transplanted to Maine—were working in offices in Portland. Daniel was an attorney and David a financial analyst. Daniel was an avid homebrewer, and David asked his brother if he'd rather spend the rest of his life in an office or brewing beer. Thankfully for Maine beer drinkers, they chose the latter.

The pair fit neatly into the ying and yang of a brewery—David took on the business side of things, and Daniel became the beer guy. Despite their natural roles, the realities of a small brewery meant a lot of work for both. In a Maine Brewer's Guild profile of Maine Beer, Dan and Dave are referred to as the "the founders, the brewmasters, the marketing directors, the CEO's, the tour guides…you get the picture." A philosophy of being small and

Maine Beer Company's new location on Route 1 in Freeport, under construction in early 2013. *Photo by the author.*

staying small kept the brewery from expanding too rapidly, but the beer's popularity has put Maine Beer on shelves in seven states.

Steady growth has allowed the brothers to bring employees into Maine Beer Company. In 2012, the brewery added brewers Kevin Glessing, Mark Fulton and Jared Carr. All three were known entities in Maine—Glessing and Fulton had worked for Sebago and Carr for Allagash.

Late in 2012, the Klehans announced they'll be moving their brewery just up the coast to Freeport. The move to a larger facility will allow Maine Beer to substantially increase production, bumping from three thousand barrels of beer a year to five thousand. At about ten thousand square feet, the new location will also allow the brewery to add a tasting room and a handful of new employees.

The brewing brothers picked "Do What's Right" as the motto for their company, and they've stuck to this simple guiding principle. Maine Beer Company's electricity is 100 percent wind power; the brewery donates all its used grain, yeast and grain bags to local farmers; and 1 percent of sales is donated to environmental nonprofits. The Dian Fossey Gorilla Fund, the Center for Wildlife and the Allied Whale Organization (based in Bar Harbor) are just a few of the organizations that have gotten beer-funded donations.

Not bad for two brothers from away.

THE BEER

Maine Beer Company's first offering, **Peeper Ale**, started out as a spring seasonal named "Spring Peeper" but proved so popular that it's now a year-round ale. An American Pale Ale in the style of West Coast brews like the Stone Pale Ale, the Spring Peeper was definitely a breath of fresh air for Maine beer locovores in 2009. Although it wasn't the only citrusy, biscuity pale ale you could buy in Maine, it was practically the only one brewed here at the time. It remains a superlative example of the style.

Lunch IPA came next and quickly shot to the top of hop-lovers' must-buy lists. A hoppy IPA with a grapefruit nose and nicely balanced bitterness, Lunch is easily among the best India Pale Ales in the country. Maine Beer has two more beers in its portfolio with a focus on hops—the amber ale **Zoe** and the pale ale **MO**, which falls somewhere between Peeper and Lunch in terms of bitterness.

Mean Old Tom is a stout, with roasted chocolate and coffee flavors balanced out by a hint of vanilla. The brewery has also released a handful of limited brews, including a barrel-aged farmhouse ale (**Thank You Allan** and a collaborative ale brewed with Vermont's Lawson's Finest Liquids named **Collaboration Time 1**).

WHAT'S IN A NAME?

Given that Maine Beer Company is a small family brewery, it should come as no surprise that a number of its beers are named for members of the Kleban line. The Zoe amber ale shares its name with David's daughter, and MO is a combination of Daniel's daughters' first initials. The brothers' uncle had a "mean smile" and inspired the Mean Old Tom stout.

Penobscot Bay Brewery

279 Main Street, Winterport | (207) 223-4500
www.winterportwinery.com | Founded 2009

THE BREWERY

Though it was founded in 2009, the story of the Penobscot Bay Brewery really starts back in 2001. That's when Mike Anderson founded the Winterport Winery. After decades of making wine at home, Anderson decided to try his hand at a bona fide commercial winery. Anderson's wines, many of them based in local Maine fruits and berries, picked up plenty of accolades over the years. By 2008, the Winterport Winery had medals from the International Eastern Wine Competition and the American Wine Society.

At the end of 2008, however, Anderson ran into a problem. Thanks to Maine's long and troubled history with prohibition, a number of odd rules governing liquor laws remained on the books. As Edgar Allen Beem wrote in *Down East Magazine* in 2010, one such rule was that wineries couldn't be granted liquor licenses. While they could offer samples on premises, they couldn't sell wine by the glass.

Winterport Winery…had a liquor license for three years by virtue of maintaining a restaurant next door (separate door, separate corporation) where it conducted wine pairings with meals and cooking classes. Owner Michael Anderson was surprised, therefore, when he was told that he would not be able to renew his license in 2009.

"Mike, we've got a problem," a state liquor inspector told him. "I want you to become a brewery."

"You what?"

It seems that Blacksmiths Winery in South Casco had applied to do what Winterport Winery was doing, and the liquor inspector in southern Maine had denied that application. "[Winterport's] license was granted erroneously," says Jeff Austin. "The inspector interpreted it as the same as a brewery."

Rather than forfeit his liquor license, Anderson bought brewing equipment. In early 2009, the Winterport Winery became the Winterport Winery and Penobscot Bay Brewery. Though one suspects that the winery is still the Andersons' passion, they've built a beer brand behind unique, well-made ales.

One particularly interesting way that Penobscot Bay has built itself into the Maine beer community is through its yearly production of "Winnah" ale. Every year, the brewery adjusts the winning recipe of the Maine Homebrewer's Competition up to a commercial scale and distributes it in kegs and twenty-two-ounce bottles. It's not just a cool piece of Maine brewing culture, but also a unique part of the national craft beer scene. The Maine Homebrewer's Competition and Sam Adams' Longshot contest are, as far as I know, the only homebrew events that award commercial-scale brewing (and distribution) to their winners.

THE BEER

The Penobscot Bay Brewery produces seven beers in all—five year-round brews and two seasonals. The brewers draw inspiration from a number of European brewing traditions, and German and English styles in particular make up most of Penobscot Bay's portfolio.

The **Wildfire Rauchbier, Humble B** and **Meadow Road Wheat Beer** all come from the German side of things. Wildfire is a smoky rauch, similar to Schlenkerla's world-class beers. Humble B is a take on the pale German lager (though it has a spicy kick thanks to added ginger and honey), and Meadow Road is a straightforward hefeweizen.

The **Old Factory Whistle Scottish Ale** and **Half Moon Stout** cover the traditional English ales. The former is a rich, caramel-flavored Scottish ale, while the latter is a full-bodied stout with the decadent flavors of roasted malt and a heady coffee aroma.

Whig Street Blonde (an American Blonde Ale) and **Red Flannel Ale** round out Penobscot's offerings. Red Flannel, an 8 percent ABV American Brown, may be the brewery's best beer. A dark, thick-tasting beer with notes of brown sugar and molasses, the strong beer is a perfect warmer for the cold Maine winter.

Baxter Brewing Company

130 Mill Street, Lewiston | (207) 333-6769
www.baxterbrewing.com | Founded 2010

THE BREWERY

Baxter Brewing came onto the beer scene in 2010 with a unique packaging twist—all of its beer would only be packaged in cans. Though other breweries in New England had played with the idea of putting their beer in cans (in Maine, the now-defunct Stone Coast comes to mind), Baxter would be the first craft brewery in New England to can its entire line of beers. It was a gamble that paid off. The brewery produced 120,000 gallons of beer in 2011, rocketing into the position of Maine's sixth-largest brewer right out of the gate.

H. Luke Livingston, the brewery's founder, took something of a sideways path into the world of brewery ownership. Before founding Baxter in 2010, Luke ran the popular beer review website BlogAboutBeer.com. Though the idea of opening a brewery was in his head—it's a pipe dream for many of us beer writers, after all—it wasn't until his mother passed away in early 2009 that he decided to chase his dream. After crafting a business plan and a year of raising capital, everything was finally set for Livingston to bring Baxter to life. Michael LaCharite (co-founder of Casco Bay Brewing Co.) was brought on board as Baxter's first brewmaster, and Baxter Brewing broke ground in Lewiston in early 2010.

Baxter's brewhouse, still under construction in 2010. *Photo by the author.*

It's impossible to talk about Baxter Brewing without discussing its location, the 160-year-old Bates Mill. The building was built in 1850 and at one time was the largest employer in the state. Like many mills in central Maine, it faced a steady decline in the twentieth century. Thanks to a less-than-stellar start to the mill's second century, it took Baxter $1.3 million and five months of renovating to prep the space for a brewery. Due to Baxter's growth, walls at the 7,400-square-foot brewery had to come down again in the summer of 2011 to increase capacity.

According to Livingston, the renovations were worth it. Sustainability has been central to the brewery's mission, and the founder told the *Sun Journal* that breathing life back into the mill was the ultimate green project.

In October 2012, Baxter announced a massive expansion to the brewery—growing from eight thousand barrels to more than thirty-three thousand barrels by the time the expansion is complete. The move will also shift Baxter to a twenty-four-hour brewing schedule, pumping out beer at an increased rate.

THE BEER

In 2011, Baxter launched with a single beer—the **Pamola Xtra Pale Ale**. The name fits the beer, a super-light pale ale with just a kiss of hops. It was quickly followed by **Stowaway IPA**, a hop-forward India Pale Ale that draws inspiration from the citrusy IPAs of the West Coast. Before the end of the year, the brewery added its first malt-forward beer, **Amber Road**.

Baxter's first seasonal ales arrived in 2012, under the stewardship of new head brewer Ben Low. Low has already proven to be one of Maine's most experimental brew masters, using unique blends of atypical ingredients to spice up the beers. **Summer Swelter Ale**, for example, is an unfiltered ale brewed with lemon and lime peel, Kaffir lime leaves and lemongrass. The mix gives the beer an almost tropical flavor—not something you'd expect from a Maine-brewed ale. Baxter's fall seasonal, **Hayride Autumn Ale**, fails to fit into any particular style. A toasted malt and rye base are accented by a blend of New Zealand hops, ginger, black pepper and orange peel, and the whole thing is cold-conditioned on oak. A Foreign Extra Stout brewed with vanilla beans and cocoa nibs, the seasonal **Phantom Punch Winter Stout** is the maltiest beer in Baxter's line and definitely hearty at 6.8 percent ABV.

WHAT'S IN A NAME?

Baxter Brewing is named for Maine's Baxter State Park. The park, which is over 200,000 acres in size, is the home of Mount Katahdin—Maine's highest peak—and the northern terminus of the Appalachian Trail. Pamola Xtra Pale Ale takes its name from the Penobscot Indian's bird spirit who is said to inhabit Katahdin. An illustration of the moose-headed Pamola is incorporated into Baxter's logo.

Oxbow Brewing Company

274 Jones Woods Road, Newcastle | (207) 315-5962
www.oxbowbeer.com | Founded 2010

THE BREWERY

"Loud beer from a quiet place" is the totally appropriate motto of Maine's American Farmhouse Brewery. The unique brewhouse, located in the middle of the woods in Newcastle, is raising a ruckus with beer drinkers around the state and from away.

Calling Oxbow a farmhouse brewery isn't just marketing meant to stir up rustic imagery. Oxbow is, quite literally, a brewery built on an eighteen-acre Maine farmstead. It's the product of years of experience in the world of beer from co-founders Tim Adams and Geoff Masland. Adams got an early start with his beer fandom, working as a bartender in Tokyo before coming back to the United States for college. Adams chose Colorado for school, where he fell in love with the region's hopping craft beer scene. It was as a young college homebrewer at Colorado College where Tim met Geoff and Dash Masland.

While Tim kept up his homebrewing habit, Geoff worked at Maine's Peak Organic Brewing with Jon Cadoux. Geoff Masland was "Partnership Maestro" at Peak, a fancy term for regional sales and marketing manager. Inspired by all the different beers and breweries he saw in Maine and on the

Image courtesy of Oxbow Brewing Company.

road, Masland hoped to start a brewery of his own. When Yarmouth native Adams moved back to Maine, he and Geoff decided to make a go of things and start their own business.

The duo converted a barn on Masland's farm into the Oxbow brewhouse, breaking ground in the winter of 2010. While they brewed test batches and honed in on the perfect Oxbow beer, they wrote business plans and got state and federal licenses. Geoff's wife, Dash, came on board, acting as office and finance manager. By July 2011, Oxbow had brewed its first beer.

Inspired by the farmhouse beers of Belgium and France, Oxbow brews exclusively with funky saison yeast. Marrying the old-world yeast with the big, bold style of American brewing, the brewery has made some truly inspired ales. Oxbow has developed a national reputation, despite the fact that its beer is only available in about four dozen bars between Camden and Kittery. Tim was named to *All About Beer Magazine*'s "30 Brewers Under Thirty" in 2013, and

Oxbow's brewery, tucked away on a bucolic Newcastle farm. *Photo courtesy of Michael Donk, brewbokeh.com.*

beer fans all over the country trade for the few bottled beers that Oxbow has produced. The brewery has had measured expansion over its first few years, which included the addition of a standalone tasting room, the hiring of an assistant brewer (Mike Fava, formerly of Nodding Head Brewery) and the beginnings of a barrel-aging program for some of its beers.

For a brewery in the middle of the Newcastle woods, Oxbow hosts an impressive number of events. Among the more unique events is a hockey tourncy that the brewery hosts on a local pond, facing off against other brewers. There's also the annual "Goods from the Woods," a festival featuring local food, food carts, live music and lots of Oxbow beer.

There are no brewers in Maine who seem to be having quite as much fun as the Oxbow crew. Their enthusiasm for their craft, and the inventive spin they put on every beer, is inspiring. Don't let the unassuming woodland digs deceive you—Oxbow is the real deal.

THE BEER

Given that Oxbow has dedicated itself to a particular school of brewing—farmhouse ales—you may worry that they exist on a very limited spectrum

Growlers allows Oxbow to sell visitors a number of different brews. In its tasting room (built in 2012), it keeps a half-dozen beers on tap. *Photo courtesy of Michael Donk, brewbokeh.com.*

of beer. Not so. Using the classic dry saison as a starting point, the crew at Oxbow has developed a wide array of unique, interesting beers.

Take, for example, the flagship **Farmhouse Pale Ale**. The FPA is kind of a hybrid of an American Pale Ale and a saison, featuring the hoppy character of a West Coast IPA and the dry, yeasty flavor of a saison. The **Oxtoberfest**, Oxbow's fall seasonal, lends the maltiness and German hops of a traditional Oktoberfest lager to a burly saison. The brewery's winter seasonal, **Saison Noel**, is a wheat-based Christmas saison and alcoholic enough to warm you up while there's snow on the ground.

Oxbow has also introduced a handful of "session" beers—brews that are light enough that drinkers can enjoy a few glasses in a single session of drinking. Given the history of saisons as beers brewed for farmhouse workers, these low-alcohol ales are right up Oxbow's alley. Its year-round **Space Cowboy Country Ale** and summer seasonal **Loretta** both clock in at under 4 percent alcohol by volume.

Finally, Oxbow's Freestyle series allows brewers Tim and Mike to stretch their creative muscles. Generally brewed a single time, these one-off beers have included a Belgian stout, a rye saison and an American IPA.

WHAT'S IN A NAME?

A number of the brewery's beers gained their names from popular music. Most people will probably recognize Space Cowboy as the best-known lyric of the Steve Miller Band song "The Joker." Freestyle #8 was nicknamed "The Chronic," and the posters for the beer's release were modeled on the art of Dr. Dre's debut album of the same name. The Loretta is brewed in the style of a grisette, a near-forgotten Belgian saison brewed for nineteenth-century coal miners. The name comes from Loretta Lynn, who famously sang that she was a "Coal Miner's Daughter."

Rising Tide Brewing Company

103 Fox Street, Portland | (207) 370-BEER
www.risingtidebrewing.com | Founded 2010

THE BREWERY

In just a few years on the craft brewing scene, Rising Tide has carved out a comfortable niche in the world of Maine brewing. The brewery, like a few of the others that have risen up in recent years, is notable for its restraint. Rising Tide brews a handful of beers; distributes only in Maine, Massachusetts, New Hampshire and Vermont; and only sends out growlers, kegs and twenty-two-ounce bombers. If the Sanborns' brewery has anything down, it's focus.

Rising Tide is the progeny of Heather and Nathan Sanborn, who released their first batch of beer in 2010. Like many in the world of Maine brewing, Nathan was a longtime homebrewer before dipping his toes into the world of craft beer. His closest brush with professional brewing was a failed application to the Stone Coast Brewing Company in 1998. In an interview with me for *RateBeer*, Sanborn credited the founders of Maine Beer Company with the final push to start a brewery. "[The Klebans] were doing pretty much exactly what I was considering and were both positive about the experience and supportive of my loose plan" to start a nanobrewery, said Sanborn.

handcrafted in Portland, Maine

Image courtesy of Rising Tide.

When his child went off to school in 2010, Nathan jumped into action—he had a formal business plan in place by February and signed a lease to a spot on Portland's Industrial Way (home to Allagash, Maine Beer and later Bull Jagger) before the end of March. The brewery opened with Nathan working every position in the brewery, with a bit of part-time help from his wife (and co-owner) Heather. Eventually, this morphed into a full-time position for Heather, described by the brewery as everything from "marketing and social media to supply chains and legal advising."

The brewery's first brewing system wasn't much larger than Sanborn's homebrew setup. A system of fifty-five-gallon kettles and a typical three-vessel system allowed Nathan to triple his batch size, but it still only netted about a barrel of Rising Tide beer per batch. The beer proved too popular for this small system to keep up with, and 2012 saw a move and expansion of the brewery. Now located on Fox Street in Portland's fast-growing Bayside neighborhood (nicknamed yEast Bayside), Rising Tide's new five-thousand-square-foot facility has dramatically increased its output. The change, from 15 barrels a month to about 120 barrels a month, allowed the brewery to expand its distribution to Massachusetts in 2012 and Vermont in 2013.

The change in venue has also allowed Rising Tide to increase its output of special brewery releases. Since moving, the Sanborns have showcased a number of single-batch brews (including a dynamite barleywine) and held their first brewery-only release: a wine barrel–aged wheat stout called Calvera.

THE BEER

Rising Tide's small stable of beers draws from brewing traditions around the world. Due to hop shortages in 2012, there are only two brews that could be called year-round offerings—**Ishmael** and **Daymark**. The former is a copper ale, an American spin on the German altbier brewed with Munich malt and American hops. The latter is an American Pale Ale brewed with locally grown rye, which gives the beer a kick of spice.

Ursa Minor is Rising Tide's first seasonal, a winter ale brewed with malted wheat, dark crystal and roasted malts to create a wheat stout. The banana flavors of a German yeast strain blend with the roasted malts to make a truly unique beer. **Atlantis**, a Black IPA, and **Zephyr**, an IPA brewed with fruity Calypso hops, were both recently available in limited quantities due to hop shortages. As the market improves, both should spin back into wider production.

The brewery has also experimented with special releases, collaborating with local businesses for limited edition beers. In 2011, a version of Ursa Minor aged in Jim Beam barrels was released as **Polaris**, with proceeds benefiting the Autism Society of Maine. Also in 2011, Rising Tide worked with their then-neighbors to brew **Prince Tuesday**, a Belgian rye ale brewed with Allagash malt and yeast, Rising Tide rye and a hop schedule designed by Maine Beer. In 2012, the Sanborns collaborated with Portland's Bard Coffee to brew **Tempest**, a coffee porter.

WHAT'S IN A NAME?

With a name like Rising Tide, it's unsurprising that many of the brewery's beers are named after nautical terms. Ishmael and Tempest take their names from Melville's and Shakespeare's seafaring fiction, for example. Ursa Minor and Polaris refer to the North Star, a nighttime navigational aid.

Bull Jagger Brewing Company

1 Industrial Way, Suite 8, Portland | (207) 838-2838
www.bulljagger.com | Founded 2011

THE BREWERY

In 2011, Tom Bull and Allan Jagger joined the myriad Maine brewers on Portland's Industrial Way. The focus of Bull Jagger is a bit different than its neighbors. While everyone else on Industrial Way has a focus on ales, Bull Jagger specializes in lagers—a class of beer styles long underrepresented by craft brewers.

Tom Bull, the brewing half of the partnership, came from a long history in Maine's brewing scene. A native of Maine's midcoast, Tom put in years as a brewer working at both Gritty McDuff's and the Stone Coast Brewpub. He also helped set up the Liberal Cup in Hallowell. Allan Jagger, a central Mainer and founder of the Maine Vintage Wood Company, took up the entrepreneurial end of the brewery.

Bull and Jagger met through mutual friends in 2009, and Allan began trying out some of Tom's homebrewed creations. Given the merits of Tom's beer—and the lack of a lager-only brewery in Maine—the two decided to move into brewing commercially. Only brewing lagers made perfect business sense, as Bull explained to MPBN's Tom Porter in 2011.

"We looked at the market, we saw what was being produced in Maine and we found that there was a hole there for lagers. Also, Alan and I prefer lagers; if you look at the largest breweries in the world, what do they brew? Budweiser, Heineken, Amstel, Stella—they're all lagers."

The pair moved into a garage space on the outskirts of Portland, joining brewing neighbors Allagash, Maine Beer, D.L. Geary and, at the time, Rising Tide. The 1,500-square-foot space fit the definition of cottage brewery, with just enough space for the pair of founders (Bull Jagger's only full-time employees) and their brewing, fermenting and bottling equipment. Still on a fairly small system, the brewery produces eight barrels of lager a week. The brewery has had the chance to expand its selection since opening and now brews four different varieties of lager.

One limit on Bull Jagger's output is the process of brewing lagers, which requires special considerations that ales do not. For one, lagers have to be fermented cold. One of the most noticeable things during a visit to the Bull Jagger brewery is the constant hum of refrigeration units, which keep the lagers at a temperature close to freezing while they are, well, lagering. The other limit on lagers is how long it takes them to come "of age"—that is, to be ready to drink. While it can take just two weeks for an ale to go from brew pot to beer glass, the time for lagers is closer to two months.

If you're looking for Bull Jagger's brews on the shelf, a packaging decision by the founders makes them instantly noticeable. Distributed in classic 16.9-ounce bottles, BJ's lagers are bigger than the typical beer bottle but smaller than a 22-ounce bomber. They are, in my experience, the perfect size for a German stein.

Unfortunately, Bull Jagger's future is up in the air. In mid-March 2013, a listing appeared on Maine's Craigslist classifieds for the brewhouse. The owners of the Big Claw brand asked Bull to work with another local brewer to brew the Big Claw pilsner, which means that the brewery's brand—if not the brewery itself—will live on. The fate of the Bull Jagger Brewing Company remains to be seen.

THE BEER

While I've mentioned that Skowhegan's Oak Pond Brewery is one of the few Maine breweries to focus heavily on lagers, Bull Jagger is unique in that it *only* brews lagers. And what lagers they are.

Bull Jagger's flagship brew is **Portland Lager**, a crisp helles lager brewed to the exacting standards of Germany's beer Purity Laws. It's simply a beautiful beer, pouring with a bright golden body and a fluffy white head. A bit more flavorful than a pilsner but similarly light and crisp, it's a perfect gateway beer for Bud and Coors drinkers.

Tom Bull's other three beers are alternative takes on the lager—certainly surprising to those that think of the mass-produced American lager as the only example of the style. **Dirigo** is a Marzen brewed in the traditional German Oktoberfest style, and **Big Claw** is a Euro pilsner brewed with European barley and Czech Saaz hops. The biggest shock of the bunch in the **Baltic Porter No. 19**. While most porters are brewed with top-fermenting ale yeast, Bull Jagger's Baltic Porter is brewed with lager yeast and then cold-conditioned for weeks. Even at 8 percent alcohol, it's a smooth drinker, featuring mellow coffee and chocolate notes before a spicy rye finish.

WHAT'S IN A NAME?

Bull Jagger's flagship brew happens to share its name with one of Maine's earliest craft beers. In the 1980s, Mainers Hugh Nazor and Jon Bove started Maine Coast Brewing in hopes of breaking into the craft beer market. Its sole beer was Portland Lager, and the bottles featured Portland Head lighthouse and a Maine schooner. While the lager was sold in sixteen states, it was ironically never made in Maine. Portland Lager was contract brewed first in northern Wisconsin and later in New York, but the operation sank before the owners could finance a brewery in Maine.

So, while Bull Jagger's Portland Lager wasn't the first beer to have that name, it was the first to actually be made in Portland.

The Boothbay Craft Brewery

301 Adams Pond Road, Boothbay | (207) 633-3411
www.boothbaycraftbrewery.com | Founded 2011

THE BREWERY

When you arrive at the Boothbay Craft Brewery, the first things you see are a one-hundred-year-old car and a two-hundred-year-old building. Next are the names of other businesses—and other breweries—plastered all over the brewhaus. They're the first signs that the BCB isn't a by-the-numbers brewery. Win Mitchell, co-founder and head brewer, will be the first to agree.

"We're kind of doing something a little different than your average brewery."

Lori and Win Mitchell, founders of the Boothbay Craft Brewery, are longtime residents of the Boothbay region. The seeds of the brewery were planted in 2005, when the couple was still running the Lobster Wharf restaurant in Southport. The restaurant was one of the first in Maine to put 60 Minute IPA on draft, and the move sparked a close friendship with Dogfish Head founder Sam Calagione. As the craft beer movement fermented in the 2000s, the couple bought the Vintage House in Boothbay with designs on creating a brewpub and craft beer destination.

More than a little inspiration was taken from Calagione, who remains a close friend and sage adviser to the Mitchells.

Image courtesy of the Boothbay Craft Brewery.

Construction of the Boothbay Craft Brewery was completed in 2011, and Boothbay joined Maine's increasingly crowded beer scene. The explosion of artisan breweries in the Pine Tree State isn't a bad thing—the Mitchells are quick to note that their brewery wouldn't exist without the help of others in the industry.

"The whole philosophy behind the Boothbay Craft Brewery is the collaboration in the industry and among businesses in our community," noted Win. Brewers from Maine and beyond have pitched in throughout the development of Boothbay's new brewery, sometimes with physical contributions and often simply with advice and encouragement.

The collaborative attitude at the Boothbay Craft Brewery goes far beyond lip service. When I toured the brewery, Win and Lori pointed out again and again the pieces provided by locals and other brewers.

The shingles on the side of the brewhaus were donated by locals George and Naomi Whitten. Matt Cole, an area builder, donated some beams for the building and some crew members to help shingle the place. Fellow Lincoln County business Barry Concrete poured the cement floor, and even the brewery's mascot—a 1928 Model T Ford—was donated by local Frank Fassett. The rooftop cupola came from down the road in Portland and can be seen from the road; the brewer plans on shining different colored lights through the glass depending on what's fermenting.

Even the keystone for the Rumford oven in the back of the brewery came from Win and Lori's uncle, a donation that earned him free pizza for life.

The skeleton of the two-story building, built with classic heavy post and beam construction, is perhaps the strongest testament to the community spirit. All the timber in the building (sawed by the Mitchells—one of the fringe benefits of having a sawmill) is from fallen trees, so no trees were cut to make the brewery. Every beam belongs to an individual, a family or other businesses, mostly from the Boothbay region but some from as far away as Massachusetts.

The beams that built the brewery were made from wood donated by friends and colleagues, including this post from Allagash's Rob Tod. *Photo by the author.*

Rob Tod donated some trees from behind Allagash Brewing, and the local Hyde School (which the Mitchells' son attends) threw in a few. Another came from just down the street at Smuttynose. Scores of local families gave up fallen trees for the brewery—many were happy to clear out the lumber. Most every beam in the brewery is softwood spruce and pine, though one of the only hardwoods came from the "off-centered" Calagiones.

Every beam and every post has the donor's name carved into its side so that visitors can see how a community came together to make this place a reality.

As for brewing credentials, Win is a longtime homebrewer who graduated from the Siebel Institute of Technology's Master Brewer program. He's also spent some time brewing at Dogfish Head, another benefit of friendship with the Calagiones. In terms of capacity, the brewery holds two ten-barrel fermenters.

THE BEER

The Boothbay Craft Brewery's flagship is the **633 American Pale Ale**, a pale ale hopped with cascade and centennial hops. With an amber body and a refreshing Cascade nose, the 633 is a quintessential American Pale Ale. It would be right at home next to the iconic Sierra Nevada's Pale Ale, a similarly hopped pale.

Black Rocks is a dark, rich stout, with coffee and chocolate flavors at the fore. Brewed with over three hundred pounds of base malt (a mix of caramel, chocolate, black and two-row), the brew clocks in at nearly 7 percent alcohol by volume. It was also the first Boothbay beer brewed by Lori Mitchell.

At the time of this writing, the brewery has only released one other beer. The **Gentian Dementia Copper Ale** was brewed as part of a collaboration with Sebago Brewing Company. It hits the sweet spot between a pale ale and an amber, with some of the hoppiness of the former and the sweeter malt flavor from the latter. The addition of herbs gives it a bit of a bitter kick.

WHAT'S IN A NAME?

Boothbay's 633 American Pale Ale takes its name from the local telephone exchange in Boothbay—all of Boothbay Harbor's phone numbers start with "633," just like the brewery's. The Black Rocks Stout is named for the nearby Black Rocks, a bunch of rocks at the mouth of Sheepscot Bay that are familiar to mariners. Pitch black and difficult to spot, the rocks are nearly invisible without radar.

Gentian Dementia, a collaborative effort with Sebago Brewing Company, is so named for the inclusion of gentian root in the brew. The bitter herb is well known to Mainers as one of the key ingredients in Moxie soda, one of the state's better-known exports.

Bunker Brewing

122 Anderson Street, Portland | (207) 450-5014
No Website Available | Founded 2012

The Brewery

Given the state's long history with prohibition, it's no surprise that some of its brewers have flirted with illicit beer production. Bunker Brewing's co-owner and head brewer Chresten Sorenson is one such outlaw brewer. Before coming to Maine, Sorenson sold beer he brewed in his Chicago apartment all over the city. Since coming to Maine, Chresten has gone straight.

After moving to Maine, Sorenson started working as a bread baker for Jay Villani, owner of a few popular Portland restaurants. After the avid homebrewer shared a few beers with his boss, conversation quickly moved to the idea of a commercial brewery. Sorenson and Villani formed a partnership, with Jay covering the real estate and permitting end and Chresten making the beer. Bunker's mission statement was a slightly Americanized take on the German Reinheitsgebot (or Beer Purity Law)—a pledge to use only "Malt, Water, Hops, Yeast, Time, Temperature and the Passion to make a damn fine glass of beer."

As for Bunker's home, the pair chose a small brick building hidden off of Portland's Anderson Street. In the fall and early winter of 2011, a former scrap yard building was transformed into an industrial-tinged cottage

Bunker founder Chresten Sorenson (right) and Maine brewing mainstay Michael LaCharite (left) pose in Bunker's one-room brewhouse. *Photo courtesy of Will Pratt, Bunker Brewing.*

brewery. Bunker's original fifty-five-gallon kettle system was a testament to the interconnectedness of Maine brewing—when Maine Beer Company upgraded to a larger system in 2011, Bunker purchased its old gear. In the summer of 2012, the delivery and installation of a 3.5-barrel brewhouse doubled Bunker's production.

Though Bunker is co-owned by Villani and Sorenson, it's basically a one-man operation. If you happen by the Anderson Street brewery, you're likely to find Chresten, putting in one of his many twelve-hour days brewing and kegging. Despite the expansion and increased production, he's still the man behind Bunker's beers. Villani's co-ownership came into play in a different way—providing a regular home for Sorenson's beers. Sonny's and Local 188 in Portland, both owned by Villani, each have two dedicated Bunker taps.

Bunker is one of many businesses that make up "yEast Bayside," an affectionate name for the fermentory businesses that have taken up residency in the Portland neighborhood. Just a few years ago, East Bayside was an unattractive cluster of industrial properties. By the end of 2012, it was home to the Bunker and Rising Tide breweries, as well as cider and kombucha crafters Urban Farm Fermentory. Tandem Coffee Roasters are also in the neighborhood, and a distillery, bakery and cheese creamery are all planned for 2013. It's a perfect partner to the breweries clustered on Portland's Industrial Way; both allow visitors to hit multiple breweries in a single stop.

THE BEER

One of the pleasures of following Bunker's birth and growth has been seeing Sorenson experiment with different styles. While there are a handful of brews that Bunker puts out regularly, it feels like every week there's something brand-new (and sometimes quite experimental) on draft at the brewhouse.

The first two beers Bunker put out—something of a proof of concept—were **Bunker Lager 1** and **Bunker Ale 2**. Both were slightly off-center takes on traditional lager and ale, a trend that has continued as the brewery has grown. Later offerings have included the **Riff Raff Rye Lager**, a few IPAs (**Green Mind**, **Beast Coast** and an **Unfiltered IPA**) and the **Magma Cascadian Dark Ale**, a hoppy brew made with dark roasted malt. On the wilder side, the brewery has crafted an imperial version of the classic Dry Irish Stout called **Trashmaster**, as well as the unique **122 IPA**, an India Pale Ale brewed with locally roasted Tandem Coffee.

My favorite of the Bunker brews is **Munjoy Mild**, a low-gravity ale with a predominantly malty palate. Despite the preponderance of English-styled breweries in Maine, very few make a flavorful, low-alcohol beer like this. It's a pitch-perfect session ale, built for enjoying over hours and hours in a pub—or at home.

WHAT'S IN A NAME?

Munjoy Hill, a historically Irish-American neighborhood on the east end of Portland, rises up practically from Bunker's front door. The popular, quickly growing section of the city is the namesake of Munjoy Mild.

Geaghan Brothers Brewing

570 Main Street, Bangor | (207) 945-3730
www.geaghanspub.com | Founded December 2011

THE BREWERY

In 1975—when Maine's craft beer scene was still a decade hence—John Geaghan founded Geaghan's Pub. It was only after three decades and three generations of family ownership that the idea of an on-site brewery began to percolate.

Early in 2010, Larry and Peter Geaghan (grandsons of John) began exploring the idea of adding a brewery to Geaghan's Pub. It's an idea the pair had been considering for some time; Maine's continuing enthusiasm for craft beer and the pub's growing popularity pushed them into action. The brothers brought in Larry's son Andrew, who started in a consulting role that soon changed to a full-time position. As the brewery steadily moved from concept toward reality, Andy brought his pal Jason Courtney on as brewmaster.

Jason Courtney was more than just a friend—he was an award-winning craft brewer. An Orrington native, Courtney spent years as a homebrewer and professional brewer in the western United States before returning to Maine. In that time, he racked up three gold medals, two bronzes and a silver at the Great American Beer Fest and silver and bronze medals at the

Image courtesy of Geaghan's Pub.

World Beer Cup. In 2002, Courtney was even named Brewmaster of the Year at the GABF. It's not a stretch to call Jason a brewing savant. It was pure luck that brought Courtney and Geaghan together. Larry and Jason's wife, Sarah, were old friends who ran into each other at a funeral in Maine, and the duo introduced their respective son and husband.

Despite the plan for a brewery and the addition of a brewmaster, Geaghan's still had to install its equipment. This led to an odd little quirk—the first exclusive Geaghan's beer wasn't brewed at the pub. In early 2011, Andy collaborated with Tim Gallon (owner and brewmaster at Black Bear Brewery in Orono) to brew MacGeoghegan's Irish Red.

By the second week of October in 2011, a five-barrel brewhouse was fabricated in an addition to the restaurant. On November 3, 2011, the inaugural batch of Smiling Irish Bastard was brewing away. Three other beers quickly followed into the pub's fermenters. The first four brews made their way to an appreciative public during a grand opening on December 3, 2011.

From the outside, Geaghan's is perhaps Maine's most unassuming brewery. Located on the tail end of a Fireside Inn and Suites, the pub threatens to be the typical hotel bar. A trip through the door in the hotel lobby, however, transports visitors into a comfortable Irish pub. A dark wood bar abuts cozy booths, and Irish flags are draped from the ceiling. The food is a mix of American brewpub fare, Irish classics and Maine seafood—a perfect fit for the Geaghans' colorful heritage. There's a sense that the space hasn't changed too radically in the decades since John Geaghan founded the pub, and that's just how the regular patrons seem to like it.

Jason Courtney, brewing a fresh batch of beer at Geaghan Brothers Brewing Company.
Photo courtesy of Geaghan Brothers Brewing.

Right now, the only way to buy Geaghan's beers is by the pint or growler at the pub. Though the family hasn't made plans for any further distribution, they also haven't ruled it out. Let's hope they do decide to distribute beyond the restaurant. With craft beer picking up steam in Bangor and an enthusiastic brewer at their back, Geaghan's could be Maine brewing's next big thing.

THE BEER

Like many of the new generation of brewpubs and breweries that have opened in Maine since the mid-2000s, Geaghan's has launched with a line of beers that aren't traditional English styles. The brewery's flagship ale, **Bangor Brown**, is a chocolatey ale with a distinctly American hop profile. Easy to drink but satisfyingly complex, the Bangor Brown's mass appeal is a testament to Courtney's decades of brewing experience.

Smiling Irish Bastard is an American Strong Pale Ale, stronger than a typical pale but not quite as burly as an imperial IPA or a barleywine. The copper-colored beer, heavily dosed with the grapefruit notes of Cascade hops, would be as at home in the Northwest as the Northeast. The strong pale is a marked contrast to **The Refueler**, an American Wheat Ale. Brewed with a hefeweizen yeast strain and served unfiltered, the straw-colored beer is light in body and bitterness. It is, I can attest, dangerously drinkable.

Given the cold weather that often whips through the Queen City in the colder months, it's no surprise that Geaghan's also offers some robust seasonal ales. The **Roundhouse Porter** and **Penobscot Icebreaker** are both high-alcohol treats, balanced but boozy enough to warm you up. **Dad's Oatmeal Stout**, a St. Patrick's Day special, is a roasty stout with a surprising hop bite from generous use of Chimook and U.S. Goldings hops.

What's in a Name?

As the brewing crown jewel of the Queen City, it's no surprise that the Geaghans' beers have names inspired by Bangor institutions. Smiling Irish Bastard is an affectionate tribute to Officer Bernie Welch, a legendary officer of the Bangor Police. Refueler salutes the Bangor-based 101st Air Refueling Wing of the Maine Air National Guard, while Hose 5 is named to honor the Bangor Fire Department.

Two further beers make reference to the men who worked on Bangor's rivers. The Tiger IPA is named for the Bangor Tigers, a nickname for the log drivers of Maine's past, and the Icebreaker is named for those who break up the ice that occasionally clogs the Penobscot River.

Rocky Coast Brewing

705 Main Street, Ogunquit | (207) 641-0640
www.postroadtavern.com/brewery.html | Founded 2012

THE BREWERY

Throughout this book, you can see a fairly clear chronology to the breweries of Maine. There's a first wave of brewers (Shipyard, Gritty's, Bar Harbor) that craft beers largely influenced by English ales and a second wave (Baxter, Sebago, Marshall Wharf) that take on more American and experimental beers. I find no small amount of cyclical poetry in the fact that Maine's newest brewery, Rocky Coast Brewing, is something of a return to those UK roots.

When they opened the Post Road Tavern in 2008, Jim Orser and Sarah Chalpin envisioned it as a taste of European culture for Southern Maine. Specializing in authentic English, German, Polish and Irish pub food, the restaurant quickly built a following among both tourists and summer visitors. The original menu also featured an extensive beer menu, with fourteen draft options and over twenty different kinds of bottled beer.

Post Road decided, rightfully so, that what a European-style pub really needed was some house-made beer. This came from Andy Tomlinson, an English homebrewer who found himself transplanted to Maine. Andy, who lives in Wells and works as a biochemist in Boston, came on as head brewer in 2012. By summer, the homebrewer had the chance to up the scale of his brewing a bit, with a 3.5-barrel brewhouse installed in the back of the tavern. Rocky Coast Brewing was born.

Andy takes pride in the sessionable strength of his beer, an attribute it shares with most British pub ales. The brewer also points to his use of fresh rather than recycled yeast (which he creates in his home lab) as the reason behind his beer's consistency and quality. Despite the relative infancy of the brewery, it's obvious that the longtime homebrewer knows what he's doing. In a short matter of months, Tomlinson cranked out four solid year-round brews and some creative seasonal ales.

Right now, the only way to get your taste buds on Rocky Coast beer is by visiting the Post Road Tavern. This is likely to change. Once they've got enough beer to satisfy thirsty tavern patrons, Tomlinson and company plan on having Rocky Coast brews available in twenty-two-ounce bombers and on draft all over Southern Maine.

THE BEER

Given Tomlinson's roots as an Englishman, it's not too surprising that he's chosen to focus on English-style ales at Rocky Coast. The beer menu is still a work in progress (the brewery has only been around for a few months at the time of this writing), but Andy seems to have nailed down the four year-round brews. They're all fairly light by American craft beer standards and a perfect complement to the restaurant's traditional English menu.

Vergers Tiple Pale Ale is a classic British pale, and at 4 percent alcohol, it's a perfect session beer. **Red's ESB** and **Bad Wolf Brown** are both full-bodied ales, with the former leaning more heavily on grassy British hops and the latter on chocolate and coffee malts. The menu is rounded out by **Parson's Stout**, a sweet, creamy stout that the brewery serves in a twenty-ounce imperial pint.

One of Rocky Coast's beers, **Angel's Old Fashioned**, defies categorization. The late winter seasonal is a pale ale, aged on bourbon-soaked oak chips and dry-hopped. The process provides the bitter pale with strong bourbon notes and a subtle vanilla flavor—a mix that's at home in a stout or porter, but surprising in a pale ale. Local drinkers definitely took kindly to the seasonal, which sold out in less than a month in late 2012.

With just a few months of brewing under its belt, it remains to be seen where Rocky Coast will go with its beers.

The Other Revolution

MAINE MEAD, CIDER, WINE AND SPIRITS

MAINE MEAD

Mead is an interesting alcoholic animal, living in a place somewhere between beer and wine. One of the oldest known fermented beverages, mead is made by using yeast to ferment a mix of water and honey, often with additional grains, spices or fruits added. While I think the body and mouth-feel of mead are close to wine, the ingredients (grain, honey and fruits and spices) are more similar to beer, as is the fermentation with yeast.

Maine Mead Works, which moved into a space on Anderson Street in November 2007, brought this ancient beverage to Portland. Longtime residents Eli Cayer and Ben Alexander co-founded the meadery and received help from South African mead-maker Garth Cambray. Cambray, who founded the Makana Meadery in 2001, provided design advice (as well as a yeast strain) to Cayer and Alexander. The venture has proven successful—in the years since starting Maine Mead Works, the operation moved into a larger facility on Washington Avenue and it has expanded from two different meads to nine varieties.

Fat Friar's Meadery in Newcastle is Maine's other dedicated meadery, and it tends to brew some more esoteric meads. Along with traditional semi-dry honey mead, Fat Friar's offers a Cherry Mallomel (brewed with dark cherries, similar to a Rosè) and Capsumel, a honey mead with chili peppers added.

Maine meaderies: Maine Mead Works, Fat Friar Meadery (Bartlett Maine Estate Winery and Shalom Orchard both produce mead, as well)

Maine Wine

The Maine legislature passed the "Maine Farm Winery Law" in 1983, placing the birth of the state's wine industry just a year ahead of its modern breweries. Robert Bartlett, who went on to open the Bartlett Maine Estate Winery that same year, wrote the law. The number of Maine wineries hasn't ballooned at the same pace as breweries in the succeeding decades, but the state is home to nearly twenty wineries and vineyards producing dozens of different varieties of wine.

Despite fairly fertile soil, Maine's harsh winters mean that only the hardiest varieties of grapes can survive. Maine winemakers take a couple different approaches to this problem—some supplement their own grapes with imported ones from friendlier climates, some brew a narrow range of wines tweaked to their home-grown grapes and a great number make wines primarily from local fruit rather than grapes. Apples, blueberries, pears, cranberries and raspberries can all be used to produce fruit wines, and nearly every Maine winery has at least one in its portfolio.

Maine wineries: Bar Harbor Cellars, Bartlett Maine Estate Winery, Blacksmiths Winery, Catherine Hill Winery, Cellardoor Vineyard, Prospect Hill Winery, Salmon Falls Winery, Savage Oakes Vineyard and Winery, Shalom Orchard Organic Winery, Sow's Ear Winery, Sweetgrass Farm Winery, Vintner's Cellar, Winterport Winery, Younity Winery.

Maine Cider

Interest in hard cider is surging in the United States. National cider sales were up 25 percent in 2012, a rate that beats even craft beer's ambitious growth. Cider was indeed a huge part of New England drinking culture in the early days of the country, but it was yet another casualty of aggressive prohibition laws. Following Prohibition, a combination of mass-produced lager and a switchover to sweeter dessert apples at many orchards essentially killed off hard cider in the United States. Free from national Prohibition, the United Kingdom and Europe continued producing traditional dry, tart cider—the style that's suddenly back in vogue in the United States.

There are a number of reasons for cider's resurgence. One is its reputation as a drink that appeals to women, which gets it in the hands of a demographic some brewers still have trouble reaching. Another is the fact that cider is naturally gluten-free, something very few beers can claim. Finally, cider has craft beer bars to blame. Bars like Novare Res and Nocturnem are opening up people's palates, and it's easy to find local cider on tap next to local beer.

Since cider is fermented in a manner similar to beer and wine, it's unsurprising that a number of Maine wineries and meaderies are also producing cider. Fatty Bampkins brand cider is produced by Blacksmiths Winery in South Casco, and Maine Mead Works makes a Mead-Cider hybrid called a "cyser." Urban Farm Fermentory, founded by Maine Mead co-founder Eli Cayer, produces cider along with mead and kombucha. There's a reason breweries aren't hopping on the cider wagon yet—vagaries of current Maine law prevent fruit-based alcoholic beverages and wheat/barley-based alcoholic beverages from being produced at the same address.

Maine cider houses: Fatty Bampkins, Kennebec Cider, Maine Mead Works, Urban Farm Fermentory

MAINE SPIRITS

The United States is home to about four hundred licensed distilleries, but Maine is home to a grand total of six. Among them, the distillers make a wide spectrum of spirits. Northern Maine Distilling has a singular focus—just vodka—but the remaining outfits make a mix of liquors. Freeport's Maine Distilleries crafts two vodkas (both made with Maine potatoes), as well as Cold River Gin. New England Distilling, a new arrival in Portland founded by former Allagash brewer Ned Wight, makes gin and rum. Union's Sweetgrass Winery is also home to Sweetgrass Distillery, which crafts brandy, rum and gin. Tree Spirits distills brandy and the apple liquor "applejack," and Spirits of Maine has a deep catalog of eau de vie, brandy, rum and liqueurs.

The spirit for spirits is quickly growing in Maine, particularly in Portland. The year 2012 saw the arrival of New England Distilling, and two further outfits are planned for 2013: Maine Craft Distilling in East Bayside and In'finiti Fermentation and Distillation, founded by the owners of Novare Res Bier Café on Commercial Street.

Maine distilleries: Maine Distilleries, New England Distilling, Northern Maine Distilling Co., Spirits of Maine Distillery, Sweetgrass Farm Distillery, Tree Spirits

The Future of Maine Beer

With craft beer continuing to see explosive growth around the country, it's not a surprise to see more new breweries popping up in Maine. The continued growth of the state's brewing industry is aided by a couple changes to Maine law that have increased the appeal of opening a small brewery.

One is the 2009 passage of LD 904—"An Act to Permit Brew Pubs to Sell Half-gallon Containers of Malt Liquor." In layman's terms, the law makes it possible for Maine brewpubs and breweries to sell sixty-four-ounce growlers of beer to patrons straight from the tap. It was a change to prior policy, which allowed brewpubs to sell growlers, but only through a "second entrance" like an attached shop or the pub's back door. The change made it possible for breweries that only distribute their beer in kegs—like Oxbow and Bunker—to sell beer directly to customers to drink at home.

A 2011 bill, "An Act To Amend the Liquor Laws of the State," changed the laws governing samples and "tasting rooms" at breweries. This is a significant change to prior policy only allowing small, samples at breweries. Now curious drinkers can order flights at a brewery bar, making for a more communal drinking experience than the industrial breweries of Maine's past.

Maine law also states that a "small brewery" (defined as a brewery producing less than fifty thousand gallons of beer a year) can self-distribute its beer. It removes the hurdle of teaming up with a distributor, which is an early logistical and financial hurdle for brewers around the country. Many of Maine's newest breweries self-distribute their wares, and even some established brewers like Oak Pond continue to distribute their kegs and bottles themselves.

At the time of this writing, nearly a dozen new breweries are planned for Maine. Rest assured that, by the time this book goes to print, there will be even more new brewers on the horizon.

Bissell Brothers Brewing

One of the exciting things about covering beer in 2012 is how social media has connected brewers and their fans. Take, for example, Bissell Brothers Brewing. Though the brewery is still a while from going public, constant updates from founders Peter and Noah Bissell have allowed curious drinkers to follow the process of opening a brewery from nearly day one.

Noah is something of an outlaw brewer, since he started homebrewing at age nineteen as a student at the University of Maine in Farmington. He credits the vibrant brewing culture of Portland as an inspiration to get started brewing and moved quickly from a basic homebrewing kit to a more sophisticated setup. Now that he's of age, Noah is sliding into the role of head brewer at Bissell Brothers. Peter, a photographer by trade and six years Noah's senior, defines his role as pretty much everything else—he's the businessman of the pair.

Since launching BissellBrothers.com in early 2012, Peter and Noah have been in constant contact with local beer fans both online and in person. Peter has stressed the importance of building a strong brand and great beer, and Bissell Brothers Brewing has been kept in the public eye through social media, interviews and beer samples. It's frankly astounding how many people are aware of the brewery, given the fact that it is still a ways off from selling its first beer.

Early in 2013, Peter and Noah signed the lease on a brewing space on Industrial Way. The spot has some brewing history—it's the space that Maine Beer occupied before moving to Freeport. Bissell Brothers has announced plans to self-distribute beer until at least 2015 and package it in four-packs of sixteen-ounce cans.

Funky Bow Beer Company

In 2013, Lyman's Funky Bow Beer Company will join the ranks of Maine's family brewing operations. Like Andrew's and Geaghan's, Funky Bow is the product of a father-son team. Located in a garage converted into a brewhouse, Paul and Abraham Lorrain's beer company is all set to brew—they received their Maine State brewing license in January 2013. The pair plans on producing a variety of beers in kegs and twenty-two-ounce bottles, as well as doing growler fills at the brewery.

Along with standard offerings like an IPA and a pale ale, Funky Bow has more esoteric offerings in the works. In an interview with beer blogger James Sanborn, the Lorrains noted that an oatmeal milk stout, a smoked bourbon porter and a European style saison are all in the works.

In mid-March 2013 Funky Bow began selling growlers of its first beer, the End of the Line Pale Ale.

KATAHDIN BEERS

After a short stint as head brewer at Baxter Brewing Company, longtime Maine brewer Michael LaCharite is looking to return to brewery ownership.

LaCharite is a member of the old guard of Maine brewing. Mike was winning homebrew competitions as an amateur in 1986 when the craft brewing revolution was starting and even founded a statewide homebrewers' club at the time. In the early '90s, he co-founded Casco Bay Brewing, where he remained until selling his share of ownership in 2000. LaCharite returned to beer to help create Baxter's three flagship beers and now is planning on opening a brewery of his own in Durham.

Katahdin Beers LLC, based on Pinkham Brook Road in Durham, will brew what LaCharite describes as "Belgian-style specialty beer," corked and caged like wine or champagne. The small-batch brewing seems to be a deliberate departure from the mass-appeal, widely distributed ales Michael brewed in his prior positions. As he told the *Sun Journal*, "You will not be able to buy them in Hannaford or 7-11. You won't buy them by the six-pack."

The production brewery in Durham will produce small, three-hundred-gallon batches starting in 2013. As of late 2012, Katahdin is in the middle of the long process of gaining local, state and federal approval and licenses. The town is behind the brewery—Durham granted Katahdin a conditional use permit in September 2012, which freed LaCharite to move on to state and federal approval.

PENNESSEEWASSEE BREWING COMPANY

Late in November 2012, Harrison's Lee Margolin launched Pennesseewassee Brewing Company with the release of a single flagship beer: Pennesseewassee Pale Ale. The brewery, the first in the Oxford Hills region, will distribute the pale ale in the western Maine foothills—Margolin anticipates distribution from Harrison to South Paris.

Lee is new to commercial brewing but has decades of experience as a homebrewer. He also has a background in neurophysiology and holds a master's and a PhD in biology from Northeastern—a scientific background that's sure to help with the chemical intricacies of brewing.

The new brewery is set to be one of Maine's smallest. The one-room brewery, attached to Margolin's home, houses a fermenter that can produce about fifteen gallons of beer per batch. With two batches of Pennesseewassee Pale a month, that puts the brewery's probable output at just about a dozen barrels a year.

Of course, if the flagship beer—a hybrid of American and English-style pale ales—takes off, the brewer is hoping to expand.

STRONG BREWING COMPANY

For years, community-supported agriculture—a setup where members pay farmers in advance for a share of their crops and get food in return—has been a model that allows farmers to connect with their community and hedge against costs. One Maine couple is looking to build a CSB, or community-supported brewery.

Al and Mia Strong fell in love with Maine during a visit to Bar Harbor in the '90s. The abundance of Maine craft breweries astounded the couple, natives of a state (New Jersey) where the microbrewery movement hadn't yet taken off. Like innumerable brewers before him, Al picked up Charlie Papazian's *The Joy of Home Brewing* and started brewing himself. The seeds of brewery ownership were planted, and after moving to Maine, the couple started investigating how they could finance a craft brewery in their adopted home of Sedgwick.

A CSB, they decided, would allow them to open a brewery without drowning in start-up debt. Rather than paying out in produce, Strong Brewing Company would pay in beer. In October 2012, the *Bangor Daily News*'s Mario Moretto described how shares would pay out. "A full shareholder gets 48 fills for the cost of their membership—$340 per share for a 64-ounce growler or $171 for a 32-ounce. A half shareholder pays less up front and gets 24 fills—$172 for the big growler, $87 for the small one. For those working out the math, the largest full shareholders will get 192 pints of beer."

At the time of this writing, the Strongs are well on their way to the forty-four shares they estimate they'll need for equipment, licensing and expenses. On top of selling shares, the brewery launched a Kickstarter campaign in 2013 to raise additional funds. The crowd-sourced fundraising fits with the Strongs' ethos, bringing the idea of patron support into the twenty-first century. The brewery has planned for production of a few forty-gallon batches a month, produced in a small twelve- by twenty-foot space on Sedgwick's Old Rope Ferry Road.

TOD MOTT'S NEW VENTURE

Tod Mott is one of New England's best-known brewers. After joining the Portsmouth Brewery in New Hampshire as head brewer in 2003, Mott helped create the vibrant beer culture that exists in the seacoast region today. Perhaps his biggest contribution to the craft beer scene is the limited release "Kate the Great," a Russian Imperial Stout that remains one of the most sought-after beers in the world.

In July 2012, MyBeerBuzz.com broke the news that Mott was leaving the Portsmouth Brewery to start a new brewery of his own. Two pieces of the announcement were of particular note: Tod was planning to open his new brewery here in Maine, and the brewer retained the rights to the recipe for Kate the Great (though Portsmouth will keep the name).

The brewer lives in South Berwick, and while he hopes to open his new operation there, he's looking for spots anywhere between the Berwicks and the York/Kittery area. Tom Atwell of the *Portland Press Herald* reported that the new brewery will begin with production of about five hundred barrels a year, and a (renamed) version of Kate will be among his beer portfolio. Other planned brews include an IPA, a non-imperial stout, a rye beer and a saison.

AND MORE...

At the time of this writing, there are a handful of Maine breweries in the earliest, nascent stages. Though they may have set up websites and begun brewing test batches, these breweries aren't quite as established as the ones above. They include Foundation Brewing Company in Southern Maine, Infidel Brewing in Rockport (a project from the owners of the Red Witch Home Brewing supply shop), Pint Tree State in Bangor, Pontbriand Brewing Company in Auburn and Farmington's Tumbledown Brewing.

Also in the works are In'finiti—the brewing part of the planned brewpub/ distillery from the founders of Novare Res—and Blue Current Brewery, a Maine-based sake brewer.

Appendix I
Maine's Lost Breweries

Pre-Prohibition

Bangor Soda Company
Casco Brewery
Crystal Fountain Bottling Company
Forest City Brewery
Rumery and Chase

Post-Prohibition

Berwick Brewing Company
Great Falls Brewing Company
Growstown Brewing Company
Kennebec Brewing Company
Lake St. George Brewing Company
Maine Coast Brewing Company
Narrow Gauge Brewing Company
Rocky Bay Public House and Brewing Company
Shag Rock Brewing Company
Slopes Northern Maine Restaurant and Brewing Company
Stone Coast Brewing Company
Sugarloaf Brewing Company

Casco Bay Brewing Company no longer has a home on Industrial Way—the brand is now brewed by Shipyard. *Photo courtesy of flickr user Cliff1066.*

Maine's Best Beer Bars

Coming to Maine and looking for a place to have a few pints? Here are some of the best options for beer—both local brews and stuff "from away." Among the fantastic pubs, bars and cafés are a handful of brewpubs, crafting unique ales and lagers served only from their taps.

THE BADGER CAFÉ AND PUB

289 Common Road, Union
(207) 785-3336

Tucked away in Union, about an hour and a half from Portland and a quick jump in from the coast, is one of my favorite little bars in Maine. I grew up about ten minutes outside of Union, and this café serendipitously opened during my last summer visiting home from college in 2007. Now a fixture on the Union common, the Badger is Christy and Michael Badger-Greer's little piece of craft beer heaven in the middle of the midcoast.

Michael was employed by specialty food store the Market Basket for years before opening the Badger and spent his years there as both a chef and the beer buyer for the store. He definitely put his love for and experience with craft beer into developing the beer and tap list for the Union café. A quick look at its taps shows a fantastic understanding of the mix of styles, strengths and prices that make up a strong list. Michael, Christy and the rest of the staff really know their beer and are awesome at answering questions and making suggestions if you need the help.

The quality of the food easily stands beside that of the beer. Many of the ingredients (cheese, produce, meats and wine, among other things) are produced locally, and the menu ranges from simple nachos to Pork Chop Normandy or polenta lasagna. In 2009, Mike won the first Maine "Iron Chef" competition at the Common Ground Fair, and he puts his pairing skills to the test with a number of specialty beer dinners throughout the year. And if you're one of Maine's many summer guests, the place usually has freeze-pops for fifty cents during the summer.

THE BAG AND KETTLE

9004 Main Street, Carrabassett Valley
(207) 237-2451

Bias admission time—the Bag and Kettle (or, more popularly, "the Bag") is my favorite bar on this list. Hell, it's one of my faves in the state. Located at… er, just beyond…the lower terminal of Sugarloaf's Double Runner chairlift, the Bag is the one bar on this list where you can ski right to the front door.

A decades-old member of the Sugarloaf community, the Bag offers an English-style pub experience in the resort's mountainside village. There's plenty of room, especially at the unique multiple-U-shaped bar, but the place gets pretty full on weekends at the height of ski season. Service is cheerful and quick, and the pub boasts some of the friendliest employees I've ever seen. If you're lucky, Uncle Al—Bag stalwart and famed member of the Outerspace Band—will be tending bar. The focus at the Bag is on classic pub food, though things are spiffed up a bit by an extensive in-house pizza menu.

It isn't exactly my style to let the food overshadow the beer, but I have to make an exception here. There are two things at the Bag and Kettle better than beer, and they're the Bag Burger and cheeseburger soup. The Bag Burger is quite notorious and was recently voted the best burger available in ski country by *Skiing* magazine. The cheeseburger soup, which feels like a heart attack in a bowl, is an awesome mix of thick, thick cheese and spiced hamburger meat.

When it comes to the beer options, there are more than a few interesting choices for the craft beer fan. The Bag brews half a dozen different beers in the back, from light lagers to stouts. Brews on regular rotation include an alpine raspberry ale and a beer brewed with locally roasted Carrabassett Coffee. The pick of the bunch is a malty and earthy Potato Ale, brewed with local Maine potatoes.

BOON ISLAND ALE HOUSE

124 Post Road, Wells
(207) 641-8489

Located right on Route 1 in Wells, the Boon Island Ale House is one of the first brewpubs tourists hit when they drive up the Maine coast. Located just a few miles northeast of Rocky Coast Brewing, the BIA offers four "Boon Island Ales" crafted by Oak Pond Brewing's Don Chandler. Three ales—a light ale, nut brown and IPA—and a lager provide enough variety that there's something to pair with anything on the restaurant's extensive menu.

Whereas most of Maine's brewpubs are most notable for their beer, the star at the Boon Island Ale House is definitely the food. The menu is understandably seafood-heavy, with all the fish and lobster sourced from New England fishermen. There's a great salad menu for folks looking for lighter fare and a burger menu loaded with huge half-pound Angus burgers.

Boon Island doesn't sell any of its beer in growlers, unfortunately. Its four brews aren't technically brewed at the restaurant, a requirement under Maine law for growler fills. When I spoke with the bartender in early 2013, he mentioned that the pub is looking at ways to make growlers available for customers "possibly as soon as this summer."

I'm hopeful that I'll be able to bring Boon Island Ale home soon. I wouldn't expect anything less from a brewpub that's self-described as "to the locals, for the locals, and all those who want to be local."

EBENEZER'S PUB

44 Allen Road, Lovell
(207) 925-3200

First off, let me straighten out one thing about the bar that confused me for years— it isn't named after Ebenezer Scrooge.

"The pub actually takes its name from George Ebenezer Kezar, a trapper

Ebenezer's. *Photo courtesy of flickr user Bernt Rostad.*

from Canterbury, New Hampshire, who came to this area in 1766," co-owner Jen Lively told the *Advertiser Democrat* in 2011. "Local lore has it that Ebenezer got in a wrestling match with a black bear, and this bear had attitude—unfortunately not as much as Ebenezer. Legend has it that Ebenezer killed the bear, but he lost one of his arms in the process."

OK, now that we have that out of the way…

When they bought Ebenezer's in 2004, Chris and Jen Lively's goal was to build the best beer bar in the world. While taste is subjective, they seem to have come pretty close to hitting that goal. When you enter the bar, you might notice a sign over the door that tosses out some of its awards. These include number one ratings from RateBeer and an astounding five-year run on "best beer bar in the world" from Beer Advocate Magazine. It's also in Lovell, a town in the middle of nowhere with a population of less than one thousand.

Though there's a great selection of imports from around the world and domestic craft beer, the Livelys put the focus squarely on Belgian brews. Ebenezer's has thirty-five taps, and you'll often find stuff that would be tough to spot anywhere else. United States' rarities and foreign treats abound.

If that's not enough, the bottle list (drawing from the pub's infamous cellar) numbers in the thousands. If it can make it to the States, you best believe it'll be at Ebenezer's, which has the best selection of gueuzes I've ever seen. The pub cheekily notes on its website that, if you're so inclined, you can also order a humble Budweiser at the pub.

The bar itself is unassuming, with a dining room that feels like it couldn't fit more than a couple dozen people comfortably. The menu is eclectic, with Maine red hot dogs and nachos sharing space with coconut shrimp, steak from locally raised beef and lobster. The staff is charming and cheerful and knows the hell out of their beer. Everything comes in the proper danged glassware. If 'Nezer's only had good beer, it would still be worth the trip, but all the trappings around it make the place world-class.

FEDERAL JACK'S

8 Western Avenue, Kennebunk
(207) 967-4322

Federal Jack's isn't just a great brewpub—it's an important part of Maine's brewing history. The brewpub was opened in 1992 by Fred Forsley and Maine brewing pioneer Alan Pugsley. This was after Alan had left Geary's Brewing to run Pugsley Brewing Systems International, but before the birth of his brewing behemoth Shipyard Brewing Company. Pugsley set up a brewing system in the Kennebunk brewpub, and his ales proved so popular that in just two years he opened a package brewery (the aforementioned Shipyard) in Portland to meet demand.

The brews available at Federal Jack's—like Export Ale, Blue Fin Stout and Old Thumper—are instantly familiar to any Maine drinker. They're Shipyard beers! However, the brews served at Federal Jack's aren't brewed at the Portland brewery. Just as they were when the pub opened in 1992, all the ales on draft at Jack's are brewed on the pub's seven-barrel system. In addition to the Shipyard recipes, the brewpub has a number of unique one-off and house beers available on draft and in growlers. For folks who are a bit bored with the Shipyard beers, the Kennebunkport Brewing Company beers offer some welcome variety. One of my favorites in recent years is Rye Tide, rye ale with a spiciness that effectively balances the signature Ringwood yeast strain.

The pub itself is idyllic, which is unsurprising considering its home in one of Maine's prettiest towns. The two-story building sits on the banks of the Kennebunk River, and a large deck and big windows offer great views from everywhere in the restaurant. A recent renovation expanded the upstairs deck and added an outdoor lounge, complete with couches and a limited menu.

Downstairs from the restaurant is KBC's seven-barrel system, which is glassed-in and visible to customers. The Lower Deck Cafe is also downstairs and serves coffee and sandwiches (and cold beer, of course). Opposite the brewhouse, there's a gift shop with loads of Shipyard swag—as well as bottles of Shipyard beer and growlers of KBC beer to go.

THE GREAT LOST BEAR

540 Forest Avenue, Portland
(207) 772-0300

It is terribly hard to think of something to say about the Great Lost Bear (GLB) that hasn't already been said.

Now in its thirty-third year, the GLB is an institution on the Maine beer scene. Since opening in 1979, the beer selection has steadily expanded— from eight beer taps to twenty-four, then thirty-six, and now sixty-nine taps. Five of these taps make up "Allagash Alley," a dedicated section of the lineup for brews on tap from Maine's Allagash Brewing. The other sixty host a rotating selection of beers from around the world, although at least a third are always devoted to Maine-brewed beer. It also has four different casks, usually featuring local brews.

Every Monday and Tuesday at the Bear is "short beer" night, with twenty-three-ounce pours for the price of a pint. Thursdays are "showcase" nights, and every Thursday the GLB hosts an event with cheap pours from a brewery or of a style of beer. Thursday nights are always a blast, and beer celebs like Garrett Oliver, Sam Calagione and Rob Tod have been known to work the taps when their brewery is featured.

As for the non-beer part of the experience, the Bear satisfies. Food is American bar fare, with some of the best burgers in Portland along with plenty of salads, sandwiches, specials and vegetarian options. The newest regular menu option is a beast worthy of *Man vs. Food*: the Cheesus Burger (a burger sandwiched between two grilled cheese sandwiches) is as extreme as any of the beers on the menu. Prices are about what you'd expect for a Portland restaurant (eight to twelve bucks for most of the entrees), and portions are massive.

There are a lot of comments deriding the service at the Great Lost Bear, and I'll go right ahead and say the service isn't fast. Still, I wouldn't say it's bad. I've been going almost weekly for the last three years (a benefit of having lived two blocks away), and the staff has always been attentive, friendly and quick to attend to our needs. It's just kind of slow. If you don't come expecting to speed in and out, your expectations won't be dashed.

THE LION'S PRIDE

112 Pleasant Street, Brunswick
(207) 373-1840

Maine is flush with "sister" breweries and brewpubs. The Liberal Cup and Run of the Mill are linked, as are Sea Dog and Shipyard. The Lion's Pride is part of one of these arrangements—the pub is owned by Ebenezer's proprietors Chris and Jen Lively. When the restaurant opened, Lively described it to the *Bowdoin Orient* as a hipper, more upscale version of his original pub.

Since opening in Brunswick in 2009, the Lion's Pride has impressed with an incredible draft beer selection. Like Ebenezer's, the pub has a reliable mix of imported treats and great American craft beers. You can frequently find offerings from Gulpener Bierbrouwerij, Hantverksbryggeriet, Schlossbrauerei Au and other consonant-heavy European breweries. These beers, rare at even great beer bars, often occupy some of the thirty-five taps at the Lion's Pride. Even rarer are beers from the pub's pilot brewing system, where special guest brewers can create unique beers that go straight to the Pride's taps. There's also an extensive bottle collection, nicely arranged in glass-front coolers behind the bar.

The pub has a dark, cozy atmosphere. Dark wood surrounds a copper-top bar, and signs for American and European breweries (some commercial, some handmade) cover the walls. The most striking part of the bar, however, is the tap handles. Rather than use the regular handles put out by the breweries, the Lion's Pride has thirty-five beautiful hand-blown glass tap handles. Illuminated from behind by shiny copper, the tap handles are works of art worthy of the well-crafted beer they pour.

Within walking distance of the Bowdoin college campus and only a short drive from Portland, the Lion's Pride is a bit more accessible than its sister pub in Lovell. The Livelys capitalize on this by keeping a busy events schedule. Along with special festivals and tap takeovers, the pub holds a weekly "Beer 101" tasting class to educate visiting drinkers.

MAMA'S CROWBAR

189 Congress Street, Portland
(207) 773-9230

Despite the strength of the Portland beer scene, the city's East End offered little for beer-lovers for ages. Thankfully, Mama's Crowbar offers an oasis for those searching to whet their whistles.

Over the years, 189 Congress has held a number of bars—for decades it was George's on the Hill, and in the early 2000s, it was Awful Annie's. Neither bar distinguished itself with its beer selection. In 2009, Patricia Pryce-Henley took over Annie's and changed the name to Mama's Crowbar. By 2010, Henley had quit her day job at the Rosemont Market to work at Mama's full time.

The inside of Mama's—a tin ceiling, barrel tables, a well-stocked shelf of books and board games—screams "dive bar" in the best way possible.

The bar is cash-only and beer-only, a policy that serves the dual purpose of keeping one kind of riff-raff out and drawing in another. Mama's hosts six taps, all of which are usually serving Maine beer. Oxbow, Rising Tide, Bunker and Allagash seem to have permanent homes on the tap list, though other breweries from Maine and "from away" do pop up. A daily happy hour drops the price of all the taps to four dollars (a steal for some of the more esoteric offerings), and daily specials on draft and bottled beer keep things reasonable.

Part of the charm of Mama's Crowbar is the eclectic series of events the bar hosts. Along with tap takeovers by Maine brewers and special releases (Mama's hosted release parties for Bunker's Trashmaster and the collaborative Prince Tuesday, for example), events range from live piano players—requests only cost a dollar!—to poetry slams to readings from local authors.

Mama's Crowbar draws a unique crowd, even for Portland. Local artists, musicians and authors mingle with professionals slowly gentrifying Munjoy Hill. Whether the bar is packed for an event or it's simply you and the bartender, Mama's feels warm and welcoming. If there's any bar in Maine that feels like your personal *Cheers*, this is it.

NOCTURNEM DRAFT HAUS

56 Main Street, Bangor
(207) 907-4380

It's about damn time Maine's third-largest city got a proper beer bar.

Nocturnem Draft Haus founder Gene Beck worked in Bangor's restaurant business since the '90s, building a dynamite selection of beer at Swett's Hogan Road Deli. A beer geek with aspirations of opening a beer-centric bar in the Queen City, Beck finally made the leap and opened Nocturnem in 2011. The project was helped along by Beck's business partner, Ann Marie Orr. Orr is a caterer by trade, so the partnership made perfect sense—he runs the bar end of things, and she runs the restaurant.

Brick walls, tile floors and a dark wooden bar make for a space that feels lived-in and comfortable, a feat considering the bar has been open for only a year. Though it's never overcrowded, Beck's bar always does seem busy. There's nothing else like it on Main Street in Bangor (the Old Port it ain't), and it's become a popular haunt for locals looking for a good glass of beer.

With fourteen taps that are constantly changing, Nocturnem serves an incredible variety of beer. There isn't a particular regional or national focus to the beer on draft or in bottles. German lagers and Belgian abbey ales rub elbows with beer from Maine, New York and California. The focus is definitely on the beer, but there is a small selection of wine, mead and cider available for folks who would rather have a different libation. There's also a thoughtful food menu, with plenty of small plates that pair well with beer and a handful of more substantial main dishes like brats, steak and burgers.

One special contribution Nocturnem has made to the Maine craft beer community is its sponsorship, along with Bangor Wine and Cheese and Central Street Farmhouse, of an annual Maine Homebrewer's Competition. The contest, which started in 2011, draws homebrew competitors from as far as Vermont and Canada. Along with bragging rights, top winners have their homebrews commercially reproduced and sold by Penobscot Bay Brewing or the Black Bear Brewery.

NOVARE RES BIER CAFÉ

4 Canal Plaza, Portland
(207) 761-2437

In 2008, Eric Michaud opened one of the most unique bars in Portland. It's tucked away in a blink-and-you'll-miss-it spot, in the basement of an old bank between Exchange and Union Streets in the Old Port.

The inside of Novare feels like, well, a basement. However, it's the coolest basement ever. It's somewhere between a dungeon, your favorite basement rec room and an English pub. It's split into two rooms: one with some comfortable chairs and couches and one with long tables and benches that encourage chatting with your barmates. The walls are brick, and the light comes mostly from some high-set windows.

The cold storage cooler for the bottles is—no joke—an old bank vault.

If the description makes it sound a bit claustrophobia-inducing, Novare is also home to one of the largest decks in Portland, which is a beautiful thing for those Maine summer evenings. The big friendly tables outside match the ones indoors, and the addition of cornhole targets and an outdoor bar have really improved the place. The service is great indoors and out, and Novare is one of the few places in the Old Port that you can grab a table and have the beer come to you.

Speaking of the beer, Novare Res is your best bet in Portland for some exemplary brews. It has twenty-five taps, two hand pumps and more than three hundred bottles to pick from. All three are rotated through regularly and offer a pretty even split of American craft brews and imported beer from Belgium, Germany, the United Kingdom and the rest of the brewing world. Novare also hosts some epic events, including annual Rogue, Smuttynose and Dogfish showcases. All the events are great for even the stingiest beer lover, with cut-rate sample and half-pint glasses.

For the ambitious drinker, Novare is also home to "The Uprising"—a list of 230-plus beers to work through that, when finished, gets you a huge chalice that you can fill with anything on tap for the price of a normal pour.

You might not be thinking much about food with all the beer to whet your appetite, but Novare is no slouch in that department either. Though the menu was a bit slim when the place opened, it has since expanded into a completely satisfying selection of snacks and small plates. It's not a place to go for a meal—the beer still takes center stage—but there's more than enough options to nom on if you're peckish.

In March 2013, Michaud's new venture opened. Located just a few blocks away on Union Wharf, In'finiti has a focus on local food, beer and spirits. Along with locally sourced food, the restaurant brews its own beer and distills its own liquor.

Bibliography

Anderson, Will. *Beer, New England: An Affectionate Look at Our Six States' Past and Present Brews and Breweries.* Portland, ME: W. Anderson & Sons Pub., 1988.

———. *The Great State of Maine Beer Book.* Portland, ME: W. Anderson & Sons Pub., 1996.

Bernstein, Joshua M. *Brewed Awakening: Behind the Beers and Brewers Leading the World's Craft Brewing Revolution.* New York: Sterling Epicure, 2011.

Clubb, Henry S. *The Maine Liquor Law: Its Origin, History, and Results, including a Life of Hon. Neal Dow.* New York: Fowler and Wells, 1856.

Cone, Kate. *What's Brewing in New England: A Guide to Brewpubs and Microbreweries.* Camden, ME: Down East, 1997.

Crouch, Andy. *The Good Beer Guide to New England.* Lebanon, NH: University Press of New England, 2006.

———. *Great American Craft Beer: A Guide to the Nation's Finest Beers and Breweries.* Philadelphia: Running, 2010.

DeBenedetti, Christian. *The Great American Ale Trail: The Craft Beer Lover's Guide to the Best Watering Holes in the Nation.* Philadelphia: Running, 2011.

Hathaway, Margaret. *Food Lovers' Guide to Maine: Best Local Specialties, Markets, Recipes, Restaurants & Events*. Guilford, CT: Globe Pequot, 2011.

Koch, Greg, and Matt Allyn. *The Brewer's Apprentice: An Insider's Guide to the Art and Craft of Beer Brewing, Taught by the Masters*. Beverly, MA: Quarry, 2011.

Miller, Norman. *Beer Lover's New England*. Guilford, CT: Globe Pequot, 2012.

Ogle, Maureen. *Ambitious Brew: The Story of American Beer*. Orlando: Harcourt, 2006.

Oliver, Garrett, ed. *The Oxford Companion to Beer*. New York: Oxford University Press, 2012.

Ward, Geoffrey C. "A Nation of Drunkards." *Prohibition*. Directed by Ken Burns and Lynn Novick. Arlington, VA: PBS, 2011. Hulu.com.

Yaeger, Brian. *Red, White, and Brew: An American Beer Odyssey*. New York: St. Martin's Griffin, 2008.

Yenne, Bill. *The Field Guide to North America's Breweries and Microbreweries*. Avenel, NJ: Crescent, 1994.

Archival material, including older volumes of the *New York Times*, *Portland Press Herald*, *Maine Sunday Telegram*, *Sun Journal* and *Kennebec Journal*, consulted at:

Bowdoin College Library, Brunswick
Glickman Library, Portland
Maine Folklife Center, Orono
Maine State Library, Augusta
Portland Public Library, Portland

Parts of this book originally appeared, in a different form, on Josh Christie's RateBeer.com blog column.

Images from Flickr are used in keeping with the creators' Creative Commons licenses.

Index

About the Author

J osh Christie's writing has appeared in print in the *Portland Phoenix*, the *Maine Sunday Telegram* and other publications and online as a featured columnist at RateBeer.com. He lives in Yarmouth, Maine, with his wife, cat and steadily growing beer cellar. Visit him at www.brewsandbooks.com.